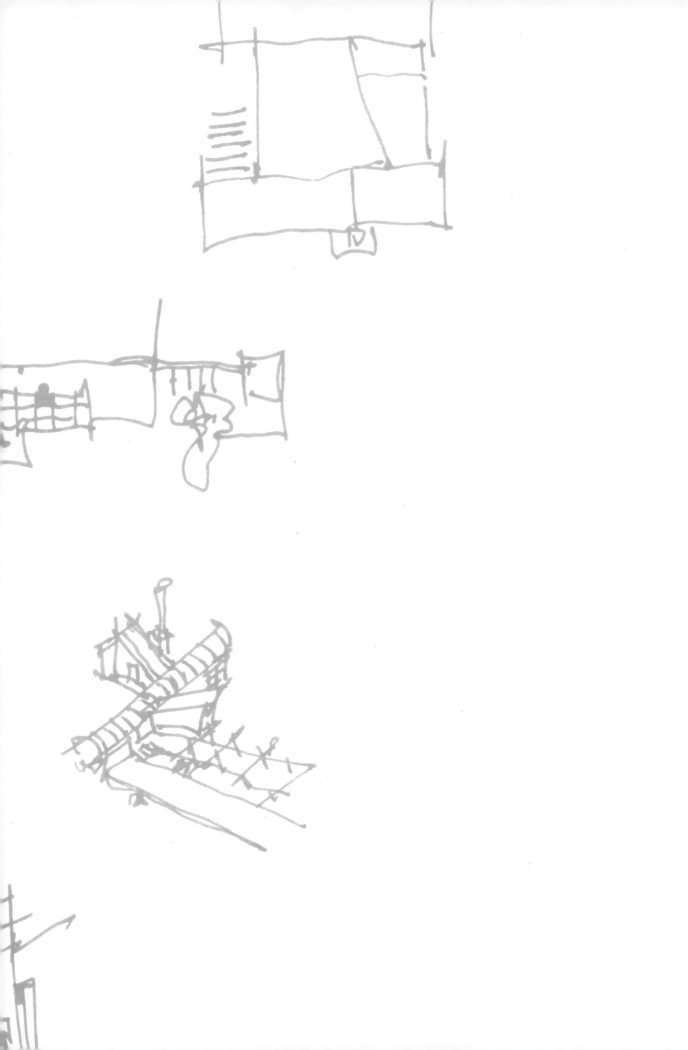

Improvisations on the Land

Houses of **Fernau+Hartman**

Richard Fernau

Essays by Beth Dunlop, Laura Hartman, Thomas Fisher, and Daniel P. Gregory

The Monacelli Press

Preface
Richard Fernau

The work presented here is the result of a long and fruitful partnership between Laura Hartman and myself. Laura had just started architecture school at the University of California, Berkeley, and I had just graduated when we met. We both shared an interest in vernacular architecture (what Joseph Esherick called "ordinary building") and have traveled extensively photographing abandoned farms, mines, trailer parks, and urban back alleys. Our collaboration began by working on a competition with one of our professors and developed later into a partnership. The houses presented here, however, are the result of nearly three decades of work and a broader collaboration with a number of talented designers with whom we have had the privilege to work.

Footings
Richard Fernau

My path to architecture was indirect, proceeding in diagonal tacks through a degree in philosophy with a minor in art, an apprenticeship in carpentry, and a short stint in art direction in Hollywood. Throughout architecture school I was uncomfortable with the idea of architecture as a fine art. The idea seemed detached and limiting but, more importantly, it ignored the vitality of the collaborative and improvisational nature of the architectural process. I was even more uncomfortable with the obfuscating language architects used to discuss their work. Despite, or perhaps because of, my aversion to architectural theory, I have been teaching, in addition to design, a course on architectural monographs and manifestoes for the last twenty years.

I was attracted to architecture as a practical art, a branch of "applied philosophy" that was not defined within the ivory tower or the art establishment. Architecture, as an art, was at best a dicey proposition, dangerously enmeshed in the compromising realities of everyday life, beyond the control of any one individual, operating in the world without a safety net. The odds seemed stacked against architecture, and the haphazard built environment seemed to confirm that architecture was anything but a pure art form. What was compelling to me nonetheless was the capacity of some buildings, even "ordinary buildings," to resist banality—to absorb compromise, if not turn it to their advantage, connecting more closely to a sense of purpose and place. This capacity was, for me, particularly evidenced in vernacular architecture, which often possesses the circumstantial quality of a design solution grounded in expediency and motivated by unselfconscious invention. Sometimes brilliant, sometimes humorous, sometimes heartbreakingly sad, the vernacular architecture that appeals to me is about solving problems within defined limits. In the most unpretentious situations (rear elevations, back alleys, loading docks, agricultural compounds), vernacular designs offer evidence, if not proof, of the potential of an overlooked means of architectural expression: the eloquence of the ordinary. Even the most basic project—a bus shelter, utility shed, or recycling facility—is located somewhere and consequently offers possibilities for transforming the experience of that place and the understanding of its function.

When I graduated from architecture school in 1974, Christo and Jeanne-Claude, environmental artists, were constructing their installation *Running Fence* across Marin County. The piece consisted of a sheet of fabric, 18 feet tall and stretching 24.5 miles across public roads, 59 private ranches, and terminating in the ocean. It had an enormous impact on me. *Running Fence* was not only incredibly beautiful—it also highlighted the sensuality, resilience, and fragility of the Northern California landscape, revealing nuances that I had overlooked. The artists' work was instrumental in helping me to define both a process and an attitude that was parallel and sympathetic to the unique conditions of the practice of architecture among the arts. Equally revelatory, however, was their inclusive attitude toward the design process and the way in which modifications to the design (implemented to meet conditions imposed by individuals, agencies, and physical circumstances) only increased the potency of the work. I began to see the architectural design process as a kind of "call and response" (performed between architect and client, architect and contractor, architect and bureaucrat) in which intentions lead to variations that lead to further improvisations. It is a process in which the telephone, as Christo observed, is just as creative a tool as the pencil. For him and Jeanne-Claude, collaboration was a given, and "compromise" was understood not as a lack of commitment, but rather as a test of creative range.

Christo and Jeanne-Claude
Running Fence
Sonoma and Marin Counties,
California, 1972–1976

The artwork of the French writer Victor Hugo, which I first encountered as a student traveling in Paris, was similarly influential. If Christo and Jeanne-Claude provided me with a model for adapting an abstract concept to a particular landscape and social reality, Hugo's experimental ink spot (*tache*) drawings provided a conceptual model for exploring a sensibility in random sets of circumstances. He created the *tache* by folding ink spots, which he would then interpret and modify to investigate various themes. In writing about Hugo's visual work, art historian Florian Rodari described his method as "steering along paths opened up by chance more or less intentionally in the direction of recognizable forms or suggestive scenes" as a means of enabling him to "tease out hidden forms in nature . . . to make unpredictable discoveries."[1]

Two ideas of Hugo's were particularly instructive. The first was the notion of using accidental circumstances to develop fresh expressions of closely held design ideas. The second was the idea of exerting a degree of control over otherwise unpredictable conditions, as in Hugo's "controlled accident" experiments, in which rather than accepting an ink spot, he attempted to shape the spot by manipulating it before it was absorbed into the paper. These experiments were for me an analogue for the architectural process, in which designers are challenged to draw their intentions out of (rather than project them onto) a mix of haphazard conditions not of their own making and over which they have only limited influence.

The *tache* can be compared to the melding of facts and forces (geographic, programmatic, and regulatory) that come together around a specific piece of ground. For us at Fernau + Hartman, a *tache*, whether it is a particular tract of land or an existing building, is a "found condition" (like the "found objects" of another of our inspirations, Robert Rauschenberg), open to reinvention. It is an aggregation of intentions, constraints, and possibilities. But because of the unpredictable nature of the architectural process — shifts in program, cuts in budget, intractable regulatory agencies, and unforeseen site conditions — we have learned that ink spots can't be trusted not to bleed, defining a new set of conditions. As a consequence, we design a certain "conceptual bagginess" into our projects to accommodate the inevitable changes and provide room to improvise on a theme, rather than be forced to dilute a rigid concept. We see the core of our work as being the choices and improvisations made within and shaped by the unique intricacies of each project's set of circumstances.

Victor Hugo
Tache from Western manuscript
1835–1863

1. Florian Rodari with Marie-Laure Prévost,
    Shadows of a Hand: The Drawings of Victor Hugo
    (New York: The Drawing Center, 1998), 48.

Field Studies
Laura Hartman

For me, becoming an architect began with just doing things I liked to do, and through circumstance and happenstance, these became what I now call "work." As a child, I spent a lot of time in the woods, damming the creek, "sailing" on large boulders, making forts behind fallen trees—unless it rained. Then it was floor plans with blocks on the basement carpet, using its gridded pattern to keep the blocks straight. The many houses under construction in my neighborhood in Charleston, West Virginia, provoked sketchbooks with floor plans of houses inhabited by invented characters. All this led me to say I was "interested" in architecture. My father, on whose back I had also drawn floor plans, cautiously encouraged me (he had wanted to be an architect), my engineer grandfather provided drafting tools, and my mother demonstrated the patience needed to make things, from model cars to wraparound skirts. Summer took us east to the beach, visiting historic buildings and gardens on the way: Monticello, Mount Vernon, and the row houses of Charleston, South Carolina, where a cottage with windows that dropped down into the wall—taken from a steamboat, it was said—fascinated me. But I was equally absorbed by the industrial structures passed along the way in West Virginia's Upper Kanawha Valley: the chemical plants belching smoke up into the sky and the conveyors and tipples bringing coal down to the trains and barges along the river. The robust explicitness of these structures, with their unabashed expression of the crude physical demands of moving material through topography, was as compelling as the lawn at the University of Virginia.

College at Smith, in Western Massachusetts, provided me with access to a very strong art department that included architectural studios and history classes within a liberal arts framework. Seminars, lectures, studios, and field trips, in architecture, geology, drawing, or photography, taught the importance of direct observation and unmediated experience, whether in encountering buildings and landscapes or in making things. To understand a place, you have to spend time there. To make things, you have to engage with the world and, as Robert Rauschenberg said, "collaborate with materials."

Attending UC Berkeley for graduate school in architecture not only introduced me to other parts of the country (I had never been west of Ohio), but also provided a social and environmental curriculum more serious, it seemed, than anything schools in the East offered. Equally intriguing was the Northern California work of Esherick Homsey Dodge & Davis and MLTW, much published at the time, with its site-sensitive informality. I met Richard Fernau not long after starting at the College of Environmental Design. Having graduated the year before, he was doing one of the things I hoped to do, designing houses. It was the mid-1970s, a hard time to find a job in an office, and Richard was piecing together a practice that quickly included a hot dog restaurant, called Franks for the Memory, and the "Working Man's White House," a private home based on his proposal for an energy conserving retrofit of the White House. His stories of the realities and complexities of the design process—of clients, local jurisdictions, and builders—gave me my first real sense of the "field conditions" of practice. Richard and I also shared two seemingly disparate but, it turned out, deeply related interests. One was in "ordinary" buildings, which led to road trips that immersed us in the vernacular structures of the West. The other was a desire to scrutinize both the interplay of formal and informal strategies and the visual consequences of the various forces at work in the design of a building. Neither interest was much a part of the conversation at school at the time, so these explorations with Richard both broadened and enriched my sense of what architecture could be.

When I decided to take a year off to work and travel, Joe Esherick, who had been my teacher, suggested that I contact his office about work. I spent a year at his firm, EHDD, which then had about twenty members, but only one other woman architect. I worked mostly with Esherick and George Homsey and got to know Chuck Davis, who has very generously provided our firm with wise counsel ever since. Nights and weekends I worked with Richard, Marvin Buchanan, and others on a competition for an energy-conserving office building in Sacramento.

After I graduated in 1978, a traveling fellowship took me to Europe, India, and then Ticino, Switzerland, to work for Dolf Schnebli's office, mostly on competitions to design schools and remodels of small stone houses in nearby mountain villages. Richard then suggested that I come work with him on the Brodhead House working drawings. After a year of working together, we formed Fernau + Hartman in 1981. In that period I was also teaching part-time at UC Berkeley, either large lecture courses on drawing or design studios. Preparing the lectures involved reading about and looking at art—particularly Marcel Duchamp, Kurt Schwitters, Robert Rauschenberg, and Richard Diebenkorn—which prompted me to regularly experiment with drawing, painting, and collage. As Fernau + Hartman grew, teaching became increasingly sporadic, but I have continued to explore the immediacy of painting and collage, and to do research on the mining structures of Appalachia in parallel with our architectural practice.

Laura Hartman
Kelly Creek, 2011

My long collaboration with Richard and with the many highly talented people who have worked with us at Fernau + Hartman has been a source of ongoing inspiration and learning. To convey the threads of exploration and to capture the spirit of our investigations and collaborations over so many years is a daunting task. I am thus particularly grateful to Richard for taking that task on in the writing of this book.

"Painting relates to both art and life. Neither can be made. I try to act in the gap between the two."[1]

Robert Rauschenberg

"Improvisation . . . it may involve the immediate composition of an entire work by its performers, or the elaboration or other variation of an existing framework, or anything in between."[2]

Barry Kernfeld

Place matters
Richard Fernau

The connection to place, which is at the center of who we are as architects, is most intense and potent in the private house. This book explores the houses of Fernau + Hartman and some of the ideas that run through them. It is about a sensibility I have developed with my partner, Laura Hartman, and other colleagues at our firm working on various building types, at a variety of scales.

The book focuses, at times, as much or more on the particular places and circumstances that gave rise to the houses (where they are located; what the land, climate, and vegetation are like; who and what influenced the design) as about architectural ideas and objects. It is about the messy process by which a team of "designers"—a team that includes not only architects and assistants, but also clients and planners, contractors and craftsmen—combine efforts, often over a number of years and considerable distances, to produce a unique, site-specific piece of architecture. The best ideas often come from unexpected directions and at awkward moments, and they do not necessarily come in the order one would choose. Designers must know how to improvise, shift their weight, respond to the unanticipated, and devise a way of working that can absorb change.

The nature of this process has always seemed to me more like that of a film writer/director than that of an outsize auteur like Howard Roark or an autonomous studio artist. All buildings contain stories worth telling, but houses are bristling with subplots, backstories, and visual detail. Architecture, however, is too complex to tell all these stories here. The improvisational and collaborative nature of the architectural process renders even the issue of authorship problematic, if not moot. A film script, no matter how carefully crafted, is reinvented by the director, reinterpreted by the actors, and restaged to meet the particular requirements of each venue. Likewise, a building is a truly collective work. We are attracted to the messy, circumstantial, "impure" quality of architecture and its inherent potential to connect us to where we are, whether that is a city, suburb, or rural site. We have developed strategies both to accommodate the unruly process and to tie a building to a particular piece of ground and the natural rhythms of the site.

Since it is not possible to tell complete stories of the houses, we must settle for vignettes. Between the common threads in this introduction and the narrative digressions that accompany each house, an image of our way of working and our sensibility will emerge.

As young designers, we asked, what if an architect's role as improviser were overt rather than covert? How would that change the process and the product? Could improvisation lead to a clearer connection to place and a richer aesthetic? Architects are closet improvisers: convention forces them to conceal the often-unplanned aspects of the architectural process and preserve the illusion of total control. But what if architecture were accepted as improvisational art?

The measure of designers' talent would then be how well they can collaborate and respond to the unexpected, rather than how well they can "hold the line" and sustain the fewest "hits" to their preconceived vision, or how well they hide the inevitable compromises. The what-if that I am suggesting is simply, "What if the role of improvisation in architecture were assumed to be fundamental?"—not a regrettable necessity, but axiomatic. What if the consequences of this process were not only part of the making, but also part of the aesthetic?

Our work often employs collage: an assemblage of diverse materials with fragments of "reality" woven in that alter the meaning of the whole and tell a more complicated story. Collage as an architectural strategy not only allows for the inclusion of disparate materials (coarse and finished) but also affords the opportunity to incorporate existing elements (fragments of structures or whole buildings) into the overall composition, to tell a story of where a house is located and how it came to be. It also explicitly addresses the reality of the design process by openly accommodating midstream changes and future additions. What appeals to us about the collage aesthetic is the ability to articulate and record choices in order to tell the story of a building's relationship to and history on the land. Architects never encounter blank canvases: they confront a unique convergence of conditions and desires.

In exploring the way collage operates, we have found particularly helpful the works of Kurt Schwitters and Robert Rauschenberg, and the attitude each had toward incorporating bits of everyday objects. Schwitters would paint over or doctor his pieces of everyday life (railway tickets, newspaper clippings) to create a more resolved whole, while Rauschenberg would often pluck objects off the street and leave them largely untouched as part of an assemblage. In designing a

Robert Rauschenberg
First Landing Jump, 1961

Kurt Schwitters
Cherry Picture, 1921

Sand City, California

Schindler House, 1922,
West Hollywood, California

house, when we are impelled to improvise—to accommodate a site condition or an unanticipated programmatic element, for example—we often choose to call out the change, as a "patch" or repair to the original design, and record it with a different material, color, or didactic detail.

For inspiration in architectural improvisation, we often look to the vernacular, which I define as the "architecture of expediency." The vernacular is not of interest for its imagery, but rather for the directness of its expression and as a source of adaptive strategies in the face of evolving circumstances. The street language of architecture, the vernacular has its own eloquence, expressing the passage of time and the decisions made along the way with unembarrassed clarity. Regional variations on vernacular architectural types (a dogtrot house or courtyard plan or Georgian hall) often offer clues to appropriate climatic responses.

Laura and I were once asked to give a lecture at the Anchorage Museum and offer suggestions about what authentic regional expression in Alaska might be. We had one day to figure this out, and we ended up showing a number of examples from a mobile home park to illustrate how, in the face of the harsh Alaskan climate, the residents had made expedient adaptations, most notably mudroom vestibules, to make their dwellings more livable. Expecting perhaps some variation on the log lodge park architecture, a significant percentage of the audience was

horrified (one woman forbade us to show our photographs outside of Alaska). Our fascination with the vernacular derives from the improvised quality of ordinary buildings; alleys are always more revealing than Main Street.

If architecture were assumed to be an improvisational art, an architect would be wise to develop informal as well as formal strategies to express the unexpected and to adapt to microclimates, hidden site conditions, and emergent environmental concerns. This kind of casual and informal sensibility has arguably always been a part of the "Bay Region style" (defined in opposition to the doctrinaire rigors of the International Style), which can be seen not only in the work of Bernard Maybeck but also continuously on through William Wurster, Joseph Esherick, Charles Moore, Donlyn Lyndon, Richard Whitaker, and William Turnbull to the present. The great critic and urbanist Lewis Mumford, who coined the term, attributed the style's origins to Berkeley at the turn of the twentieth century. He described it as a "native and humane form of modernism . . . a free yet unobtrusive expression of the terrain, the climate, and the way of life on the Coast."[3]

We have always had a slightly awkward relationship with the Bay Region style—not the tradition itself, but the regionalism that is implied in the term. It never was our intention to be regionalists, and we have been reluctant to be associated with the term. However, we have been greatly influenced by the Bay Area tradition, both by the work (which is all around us) and by its practitioners, a few of whom we studied under, worked for, or taught alongside at UC Berkeley. Eudora Welty, the renowned writer from the Mississippi Delta who was often belittled by the regionalist label, had it right when she called regionalism "an outsider's term."[4] The Delta was where she wrote from; it shaped her sensibility but her "regionalism" was a by-product of her point of view, not her goal. What sense does it make, she asked, to call Cervantes or Turgenev a regionalist? Our ambition has always been to develop a place-rooted architecture, a sensibility that would allow us to work in a variety of landscapes and climates, and the place where we were was Northern California.

My first "office" was in a garage and potting shed (where I lived) in the garden behind Maybeck's Lawson House, less than a hundred yards from where Maybeck had had his home and studio. The office was so small that working outside was an attractive option much of the year. A number of houses by well-known architects were close by, and all the generations of the Bay Area tradition were represented. Maybeck, Wurster, Esherick, Julia Morgan, and Donald Olsen (as well as notable Southern California outliers such as Rudolph Schindler) had designed houses within a quarter of a mile. Having minimal practical experience before opening an office, and not much of a portfolio to show clients, Laura and I would take them on walks through the hills at various points in the design process and talk about details and materials or the way a house was situated on its site and its relationship to the landscape. Autodidacts in the craft aspect of architecture, we found that this formative period constituted a kind of accidental apprenticeship in the Bay Region tradition. Later, when lecturing about our work outside the country, I used to begin with a slide show of architecture within a ten-minute stroll from the studio. This was meant as a way of suggesting that in addition to an architectural canon that we all share, there is a personal canon, if we are lucky, of the things that we know, admire, and see every day that shape our point of view.

Living and working in close proximity to one of Maybeck's most iconic residential works had a particularly strong influence on

us. The most commonly admired quality of his architecture—a combining of historical styles—was not what interested us. Underneath the picturesque and theatrical gestures were important lessons: the juxtaposition of heterogeneous elements; the notion of architecture telling a story, as in the "remodel aesthetic" of Charles Keeler's house; the blurring of the distinction between indoors and outdoors—and underneath the tireless invention, a certain lightness. A true bohemian, Maybeck worked outside much of the year; his summer office was under a canvas sheet. He designed houses with outdoor living rooms, showers, and sleeping porches to facilitate a similar lifestyle. Moreover, he used landscape, such as hedges and allées, and landscape elements, such as trellises, pavilions, and outdoor fireplaces, to extend his residences into their gardens, embedding the houses in their sites. Maybeck was witty, eccentric, inventive, and environmentally aware; living and working in his former backyard was infectious.

One of my earliest built projects, the Brodhead House, in La Honda, California, was commissioned as a result of an agitprop proposal to retrofit the White House. It was

1978, in the shadow of the first oil crisis. I was just out of school and Jimmy Carter was formulating an energy policy. Friends of the Earth approached me and asked if there was anything we could do to push national policy in the direction of low-tech, passive solar energy and strategies for energy conservation. In particular, I was intent on demystifying sustainability by explaining the ways in which traditional American architecture had been adapted to climate. A long night produced a one-page cartoon that listed straightforward suggestions ranging from sunshades to a greenhouse to bringing back President Wilson's idea of having sheep trim the south lawn to save gas. The proposal was sufficiently provocative at the time for the *Washington Post* to run it as a full-page spread and interview a member of the White House. At first dismissive (wondering about "people watching where they stepped" and "the sheep during the twenty-one gun salute"), a member of the White House staff later apologized in a phone call, saying they were giving the proposal serious study. Because it was timely and the press found it amusing, the story was published nationally and internationally, and the phone began to ring. I began getting calls from prospective clients. The Brodhead House was my first opportunity to explore and test these initial investigations: traditional and emerging sustainable design strategies as a means of tying a house to its site.

Although the energy conservation movement was in a nascent stage in the 1970s, it was discouraging to see that green architecture was already congealing into a style: a contradiction for architecture that was supposed to be site- and climate-specific.[5] Solar houses with concrete walls and acute triangular sections were emerging from climates as divergent as those of Switzerland, Arizona, and Hawaii. Consequently, I wanted to explore what would result if I started with a traditional house form and adapted it to the site, the climate, and the particular requirements of energy conservation. Thermally, the house combines the heating strategy of a colonial house (with its massive, centrally located fireplace) and the cooling, air-circulating properties of a Georgian plan (with its central circulation hall and belvedere). The necessary modifications to the traditional gable form are called out with material changes and are foregrounded, even caricatured, through additions to or subtractions from the basic shape. This approach is similar to the Japanese tradition of mending, in which repairs are incorporated as part of the design

La Verada, the garage where I lived and worked, and the first Fernau + Hartman office, 1982

Ernest Coxhead House, San Francisco

Sakiori and *sashiko* are Japanese traditions of mending where the repair or "patch" is foregrounded, rather than suppressed, and is integrated into the design.

and celebrated. The Brodhead House was pivotal in shaping my thinking not only in terms of site-specific, sustainable design, but also in terms of exploring the idea of a "remodel aesthetic": "patching" or "mending" initial design ideas to adapt to site-specific conditions.

Many years later, in the spring of 2000, the Architectural League of New York mounted "Ten Shades of Green," an exhibition curated by Peter Buchanan. "Ten Shades of Green" showcased contemporary architecture that "combined environmental responsibility with formal ambition"[6] and, in many ways, articulated what we had been working toward all along. The exhibition focused on large institutional projects by European architects but also included houses by four Americans. Our Straw-bale House (1995–1999) in Northern California was among them. The radical agenda of the exhibition was to unpack the notion of sustainable architecture and rescue it from being dismissed as a technological fix rather than a cultural/architectural paradigm shift. Buchanan opened the discussion to include not only sophisticated technological analyses but also a broader set of criteria, including aesthetic, environmental, social, and experiential considerations, to understand what it means to be "green." In addition to efficient systems and first principles (solar gain, sun shading, insulation, natural ventilation, and daylighting), he included: "loose fit" (buildings that age well, that people want to keep, and that can be adapted); updating the local vernacular through a contemporary lens; enhancing a sense of connection to the natural world; and increasing a sense of well-being by embedding a building in its site. Buchanan argued that for green architecture to succeed as a true paradigm shift, it must address the sensual aspects of sustainability that connect people to a particular environment.

Oscar Wilde famously observed that if

nature had been comfortable, architecture would never have been invented. Yet Herman Melville sounded a cautionary note in *Moby-Dick* on the deadening effect of the "luxurious discomforts" of too well-tempered environments that alienate us from our experience. He argued that to truly "enjoy bodily warmth, some part of you must be cold, for there is no quality in this world that is not what it is merely by contrast."[7] The question then becomes, how much architecture is required to be "comfortable" before we lose all sense of where we are? A wall? A floor? A roof? In what seasons and for what activities? Houses are ideal for exploring these issues, because there is someone, the client, there to make a decision and take a chance. Second homes, because where they are located is their reason for being, are particularly rich with possibilities. This tension between providing comfort and cutting us off from where we are and what sustains us is at the very core of what architecture is and should be.

There is no set formula for embedding a house in its site. Green architecture is not to be found in a catalog or a spec book. Degree-days, sun angles, and climate records only get you so far (usually someplace close to the airport). To marry a house to its site, you must at a minimum know the conditions on the ground year-round, and to do that you must spend time. It might entail building a platform or renting a cherry picker to confirm critical views, placing anemometers on-site to record site-specific wind data, talking with locals about snow buildup and drifts, or camping out on the site. It always entails time on the land. Nothing can substitute for direct experience.

All our buildings begin with an intensive landscape study, whether the site is a working ranch or an urban parcel. We look for ways of exiting the box, of creating both defined outdoor rooms and casual, almost accidental exterior spaces (only partially defined by

architecture and landscape features). These rooms are there to be found and invite engagement with the site and the senses. Houses in particular have given us the opportunity to explore, in strikingly different locations and climates, a variety of architectural and landscape strategies that blur the boundary between indoors and outdoors, deepening the connection between built and natural environments. These outdoor rooms not only expand the experience of a house, but also connect us to where we are.

The houses in this book are the product of collaborations between people, within a given set of circumstances, played out on a particular piece of land. Despite the massive level of planning and organization, there is a rogue element in the architectural process that demands, at odd moments, that we rethink choices and depart from the plan. While often vexatious, these moments are invariably imbued with possibilities to invent— if we are open to them. This willingness to take a chance and depart from the script to address a problem is the quality we most admire in vernacular architecture. It is often what particularizes and humanizes a building. It is our hope that our improvisations on the land share, along with architectural rigor, some spark of the vernacular pragmatism and wit. At the heart of our work is the simple belief that place matters. A house can be an instrument to connect you to where you are and, in doing so, connect you to yourself.

1. Calvin Tomkins, *The Bride and the Bachelors: Five Masters of the Avant-Garde* (New York: Penguin Books, 1976), 193.

2. Barry Kernfeld, "Improvisation," in *The New Grove Dictionary of Jazz* (New York: St. Martin's Press, 1988), 554.

3. Lewis Mumford, "The Sky Line," *The New Yorker* (October 11, 1947), 110.

4. Eudora Welty, "Place in Fiction," *The Eye of the Story* (New York: Vintage Books, 1979), 132.

5. Richard Fernau, "Solar Architecture: a New Regionalism," *Werk-Archithese*, vol. 65, 1978.

6. Rosalie Genevro, Preface, in Peter Buchanan, *Ten Shades of Green* (New York: The Architectural League of New York, 2005), 4.

7. Herman Melville, *Moby-Dick* (Berkeley and Los Angeles, CA: University of California Press, 1979 [1851]), 55.

Rooted Modernism
Beth Dunlop

Talk to Richard Fernau and Laura Hartman about architecture, and you will find yourself speaking about literature, film, philosophy—about ideas. All of these, of course, are ultimately tracked back to architecture, but theirs is a discourse—and an investigation—that explores a wide territory. They are architects with restless minds and endless curiosity, two traits that imbue even the smallest and simplest of their buildings with a richness and sense of relevance. Their firm, Fernau + Hartman, has to its credit a wide body of important, interesting, and well-recognized built work that is set apart by the fact that each building—no matter where it is, what size or shape it is, or what purpose it serves—seems fully connected to its specific terrain, to history, to culture, and, most pertinently perhaps, to the art and craft of building. There's a kind of narrative strain to each project that seems to connect back to a larger sense of the whole.

The architecture of Fernau + Hartman defies easy definition. It falls into a category that somehow transcends most definitions: it is modern, yes, but not dogmatically so; regional but hardly traditional. The work is respectful and, in some ways, even humble (in the sense that it doesn't seek to dominate its occupants or its surroundings but becomes part of the lives of both). It is serious in its purpose, yet it is also far from sober—rather, it has a sense of spontaneity and joy that eludes much of the self-conscious architecture that surrounds us today. The firm's work is true to itself, with a regard for its own origins. I like to call it "rooted modernism," meaning that each building is somehow inextricably of its own place and time.

Designing such an architecture is no easy task. There are few guidelines for making buildings that speak to what and where they are, no real rules. The journey to get there is a long one. It generally begins with a phone call, an email, or a knock on the door of their studio, but the destination is miles away, metaphorically speaking—and sometimes geographically. Theirs is architecture that reflects its site and setting, resonates with its occupants, and evokes a sense of past and present in a way that is comfortable and accessible while remaining intellectually challenging. Both architects are keen, thoughtful, and deeply introspective observers, and the process by which they design and build, connecting them to people and place, is profound.

The houses that are shown on these pages are perhaps the most personal of Fernau + Hartman's output over the past thirty-five years, but they are also representative of the rigor and romance (hardly an academic term, I admit, but apt here) that go into each of the firm's buildings. Without the former, you can't have a building that stands up or functions. Without the latter, you can't have architecture, because architecture is the three-dimensional representation of our connection to land and landscape, art and culture, history and memory—and to the possibilities that lie in the near future. Without those intangibles, all those silent forces that inform the making of a building, you would

Rendering for CuriOdyssey,
a science and wildlife center,
San Mateo, California.

Eastside School, Palo Alto,
California. Completed in 2005.

have mere structures, aggregations of wood and glass and steel, but you would not have architecture.

Both Richard Fernau and Laura Hartman live and practice in the Bay Area, so they are steeped in the traditions of Northern California. This is important to note, but like so much else in the Fernau + Hartman résumé, this geography is translated into something larger. Northern California is indeed the springboard. Much of what they know and believe about architecture is the product not only of their respective University of California at Berkeley educations, but also stems from their astute observations of the intricacies and nuances of the architecture and landscape of their hometown, the years of learning and looking. All this is so profoundly instilled in them that it has become an innate part of their design process. So Northern California shows up, definitely, but more as an approach, a philosophy, a way of problem solving, rather than as a specific aesthetic or a geographic limitation.

Indeed, the houses shown here are located across the country, from the dunes of Martha's Vineyard, the riverbanks of the Hudson River, and the rolling hills of West Virginia, to the remote mesas of the Rocky Mountains and the rugged ranchlands of Montana. There is a body of work clustered in Northern California, but a quick study reveals differences in each project, both strong and subtle. There are connections between one house and another, to be sure, found most particularly in an inclination to break a house or compound into its distinct components (all the better to live on the land), in the use of less-expected materials, and in a courageous and memorable color palette. Some of this could probably be traced back to their immediate geography, but much of it is particular to the two architects and their process. It is a process that is at once empirical and intuitive, and it often begins with one saying to the other, "Let's take a walk around."

This is more than a casual comment; rather, it is an imperative. Walking around means exactly that—a trudge across the terrain—and at the same time, it is a metaphor for the intellectual inquiry that will follow, which involves a range of disciplines: geology, horticulture, geography, art, literature. To delve into the files and minds of both architects is a trip that can cover in one breath topological studies, the writings of Eudora Welty, the collages of Robert Rauschenberg, the quilts of Gee's Bend.

Richard and Laura's exhaustive analysis ferrets out the truths, both obvious and subtle, of the land—from archeology to geology—and of the longtime man-made responses to that land that are considered to be vernacular architecture. The deep-set building traditions they seek out and study are always instructive, making up in insights offered what they might lack in modern-day aesthetic appeal. This translates into an architectural belief system that is deeply personal, but also pragmatic: a way to learn from the wisdom of those who have lived on the land without the advances that modern technology and materials have brought.

Collapsed barn and deconstructed granary in Park County, Montana, reveal overlooked properties and formal possibilities of wood construction.

A louvered colonnade on the street in Locke, California, in the Sacramento River Delta, suggests strategies for creating ambiguous indoor/outdoor spaces.

landscape. Looking back, Richard Fernau says the firm most definitely did not want to be of the "let's look like France" or "let's look like Italy" school of thought.

There has been a consistent quest for what Fernau calls "strategies of clarity," a quest that has led the architects to understand at a profound level what it means to inhabit a particular place. The clues to this understanding come, of course, from both the land and its longtime buildings (and perhaps, one might say, building culture), but the architects take such implicit ideas much further and at the same time reduce them into a legible statement. Importantly, this does not necessarily result in a direct or literal stylistic connection to the regional architectural vocabulary, at least not entirely; the forms of a particular house may recall the vernacular, but in the hands of Fernau + Hartman, they are actually new. The architects often refer to the idea of collage, a contemporary concept most often connected to Southern California architecture and the ideas expounded by Frank Israel, in particular, and found in the films and theories of Sergei Eisenstein. The comparison to collage, to the layering of images and concepts one upon another, is apt here. And if the work bends some rules of architecture, one might ask, who wrote those rules? For Fernau + Hartman, it is more a matter of creating work that makes sense.

There is an additional layer in the process, which is the client. Talk to Fernau + Hartman's clients, and they will tell a story of architects who ask penetrating questions, listen well, watch carefully. Clients describe the experience of working with Richard and Laura as being intense, exciting, and transformative. In one early commission, the Laybourne House and Art Barn (see page 48), architects and clients (Geraldine and Kit Laybourne) even camped out on the remote mesa to make sure not only of the placement of the house on the land, but also of the finite details: the position of the sunrise and the sunset, the views to each direction. After that, Richard and Laura outlined the house, relying on ancient geometries and time-tested methods, including stakes and rope, then handed Kit a small video camera and asked him to walk through the proposed layout. This was a later step in the process, however; all four had already visited the site several times and had scoured the region looking at both land and buildings to gain an understanding of this unusual site, Colorado mesa land with long views. "They grounded us," says Kit, "in ways that were both wonderfully strange and terrific." He recalls that in the hours they spent together, it became clear that the designers were delving into their clients' minds, their psyches, accumulating "loads" of information as they went along.

Basic to this is the respect both architects have for the found condition, for architecture "made by people working with minimal means," as Richard puts it. Too often, he says, when architects try to interpret the vernacular, what survives are just the "figurative aspects, the cute parts," which in turn find their way into shopping centers and entertainment complexes. By contrast, the work of Fernau + Hartman reaches far into those traditions, and while what emerges may manifest itself in specific, often recognizable forms, there's something much deeper present too, a feeling that the architects have grasped a piece of the place's soul. Fernau puts it this way: "We've hung onto a number of ideas over the years, chief of which is that place will always matter. It's been one of our touchstones"— and it is a powerful guiding principle.

In designing the Berggruen House in Napa Valley, California (see page 24), the architects sought not only to speak to the rural winemaking aesthetic (of barns and caves, barrels and staves) of Northern California but also to draw on the materials and hues, as well as the striking geometries, of the vineyard landscape. For this house, the architects took inspiration from water towers, agricultural buildings, and much more, striking out against the château mentality that was overtaking the region. Later the firm would go on to design the Napa Valley Museum, which likewise invokes the region's culture, architecture, and

Completed in 1993, this Laybourne House does draw on the gritty architecture of Colorado's long-abandoned mining camps and quite faithfully pays homage to that very particular rural-industrial legacy. But it also has a strong, lively, almost mischievous character that reflects the clients'. Richard and Laura "study the place, but they also study the clients. They studied us until they got who we were. They immersed themselves," says Geraldine. "They managed to get the spirit of Telluride and the spirit of us."

Laybourne House and Art
Barn (page 48)

From the start, Fernau + Hartman garnered a fair share of attention for creating work that was environmentally conscious, an act that stood out in the 1990s and well into the millennium. Today it is a given that well-meaning architects (which, optimistically, one would wish meant all architects) have good intentions toward nonrenewable resources; this ethos is so inculcated in the work of Fernau + Hartman that it almost doesn't bear discussion. Still, for the record, it is worth noting, for example, that the Potomac Retreat in Eastern Panhandle, West Virginia (see page 76), was built with local masons laying native limestone and local timber framers hammering West Virginia oak. The house has metal-and-wood siding, again a nod to local building practices. The firm's redesign of a historic house and reconstruction of a guest cottage in Nonquitt, Massachusetts, produced a complex that, at the owners' request, does not rely on air-conditioning but lets the breezes from Buzzards Bay in Cape Cod flow through freely (see page 142).

Again, it is much less an agenda than just a given. Richard called it at one point "an attitude toward making," pointing out that it was simply sensible to put thick walls to the north and west to avoid heat gain and to open the house with windows to the east and south for light and warmth. The greenness of Fernau + Hartman's architecture is at once imposed and innate. It is imposed in the sense that it is that way because of the acquired knowledge of what ought to be, of what is right. That it is innate, once again, comes from this thorough study of the vernacular, of the building techniques and traditions of those who had no other option but to work with local materials and within the constraints of local conditions, ranging from topography to climate.

It is an intriguing marriage of motives and methods, and it is one that seems to pervade all of the firm's work. In architecture today (and in recent decades), the choice is often an either/or—contextual or contemporary, renovate or build anew—but Fernau + Hartman has been able to bridge these gaps. The tension between old and new can pull architects in many directions, but for Richard and Laura, it is a seamless part of the practice, another path of inquiry, and yet another way to invoke that wider cultural palette, offering opportunities for metaphor: for example, in the idea of alluding to the region's whaling past (and, of course, in turn making at least an oblique allusion to *Moby Dick*) in the renovation and reuse of the house in Nonquitt. Another such project was a second house done for Geraldine and Kit Laybourne, in this case a

renovation and addition to an 1861 house overlooking the train station and the Hudson River in the working river town of Rhinecliff, New York (see page 172). The challenge there was to create an addition that maintains the character of the old house while expanding the interior to let it be entirely modern. Both architects and clients wanted to be respectful of the more unassuming local aesthetic; thus the exterior facing the street was left traditional while the modern addition cascades down the hillside a bit. Kit terms it "an honest house on the outside and on the inside."

Fernau + Hartman is often confronted with projects that involve the reuse of historic structures. The firm tends to attract clients who work in the arts or are passionate about art and likewise passionate above the environment—which in turn means that these projects involve buildings that are not merely historically interesting, but also fairly quirky. At the Avis Ranch in Montana (see page 84), the complex of century-old buildings they needed to adapt included two granaries and an outhouse. This nearly twenty-year project of renovating a rural homestead and slowly adding buildings to the site culminated in a modern ranch house, called the Cookhouse (see page 96), which is steeped in the local architectural heritage and yet very much of its own time. This long project has given the two architects a chance not only to build on a powerful tradition but also, as Laura says, "to focus on the land. We keep trying to explore where the building ends and the land begins and vice versa. What's inside and what's outside? What's that membrane?"

All of this seems to stem, quite naturally, from their profound interest in the interaction of architecture and landscape, in the planted materials that help shape the site and define the architecture. This fundamental of the practice was honed in the firm's early days, when the two architects would lead clients around the Berkeley neighborhood of their studio, thus refining their own sensibilities through observation and study. From the earliest commissions, the work of Fernau + Hartman has always entirely engaged the landscape in ways that are both creative and unexpected. In both Richard's own home and the Laybourne House in Telluride, the master bed is set on rails to roll from the enclosed bedroom out to a deck. At the Anderson/Ayers House in Marin County, California, a previously undetected spring was incorporated into the architectural ensemble as a kind of circumstantial water feature between the two principal structures in the complex (see page 118).

Realists and dreamers, Richard and Laura acknowledge—no, actually embrace—the opportunity for improvisation, a technique that is more commonly associated with theater, jazz, and modern dance. Of course, there's a difference between ephemeral moments of performance and the more permanent world of architecture. In some ways, improvisation is linked to imagination: to the realm of the what-ifs in thinking about almost anything, from siting to the selection of materials to the choice of paint colors. Architecture is often expressed in absolutes, but Richard and Laura know better. Like the spring that bubbled up on the Marin County job site, unexpected opportunities and obstacles present themselves in almost every project.

And for all that is actually problem-solving, down-to-earth, and pragmatic, in the end there is another dimension to this work that springs from this fervently intuited, often spontaneous, yet deeply felt, carefully and closely wrought course of action that takes each project from idea to reality. The work is unjaded; absent that all-too-frequent been-there-done-that cynicism that can undermine architecture and ultimately make it drab and boring, or repetitive and clichéd. There is none of that here but rather—building by building, house by house—a new sense of discovery.

Original farm worker housing, before the renovation

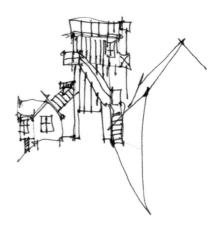

Berggruen House
Napa Valley, California, 1986–1988

This house began as a remodel. In a certain sense it still is, although only a small section of nondescript, but structurally respectable, wall remains from the original structure.

Located in Napa Valley, the center of California wine production, the site escaped cultivation by being wedged between two creeks and wooded. In all directions, views look out over geometric rows of commercial vineyards to the mountains beyond. The scene, however, changes dramatically with the cycles of production. The site is alternately experienced as crowded and noisy, or isolated and still.

Once farmworker housing, the casual collection of small, foundationless wood-and-tin structures was purchased by our client and inhabited for a number of years before she decided to remodel the house. In addition to the basic amenities of a modest home, the house had to accommodate interior and exterior workspace for two artists. Because of the site and temperate climate, and because of their predilections and preoccupations, the artists spent much of the day working, relaxing, and "commuting" between their work spaces, where various projects were underway. Like at many rural (and working) compounds, the space between the work areas was as significant as the work areas themselves.

We began by learning and salvaging from both the site and the artists' experience of it. We attempted to mend and augment the site to enhance its particularity and to offer an alternative to the dominant "Loire/Med/south-of-somewhere" style that is becoming associated with Napa Valley.

From the start, the house was to be small, composed of individual pieces similar in scale to those we found there. The original dwelling — a 9-by-29-foot gable-roofed shack with rooms arranged enfilade — had been buried under years of "improvements." Well-sited and central, this building, or more precisely its memory, became the "cookhouse" off of which we pulled the sleeping and working rooms. We maintained its typological purity but greatly increased its livability by adding a series of outshoots that extend the interior space and tie it to the site. Along with the outbuildings, these outshoots define a central yard that is accessible by truck through the entry tower that houses one of the bedrooms and a studio (as a side benefit, you can knock on the front door without getting out of your vehicle). The yard also functions as a gathering place for studio openings and is further defined on the northern edge by a small open-air lodge-like structure that encloses an outdoor hearth. Evenly spaced, mature trees lining a creek establish the eastern wall of the site.

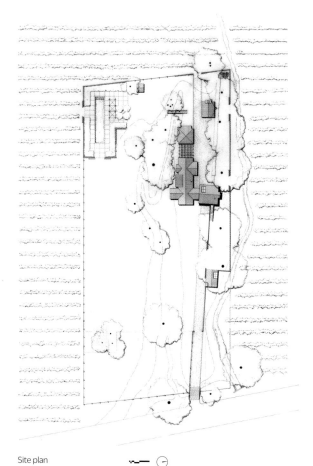

Site plan

Axonometric

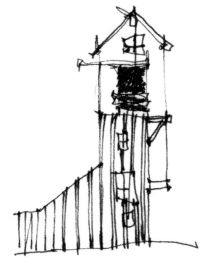

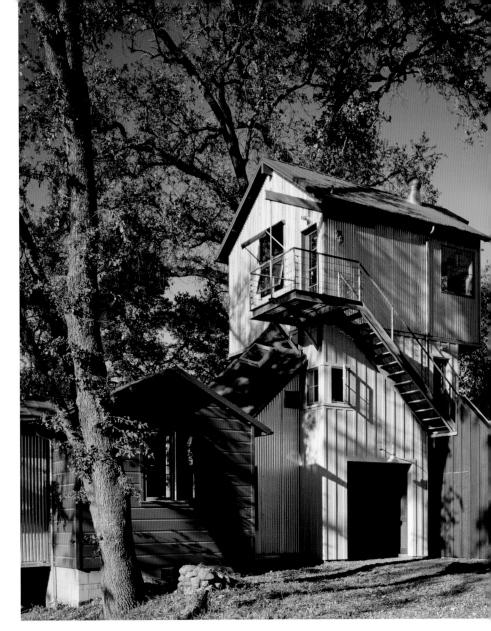

Water tower in Napa,
California

West elevation

Section through the tower

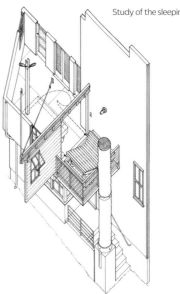

Study of the sleeping porch

Fernau/Cunniff House
Berkeley, California, 1990–1992

The original house was a tiny, undistinguished, flat-roofed modernist structure of roughly 500 square feet. (At the time my wife and I bought the house, it was the least expensive listing in north Berkeley.) A house designed in the fifties for affordability, it was originally a single large room paneled in redwood with a fireplace. The room accommodated sleeping, dining, and living, and was perched on top of a single-car garage. Running along one side of this room was a bar of service spaces: closet, bathroom, and a tiny kitchen (noted on the original drawings as the "Murphy kitchen"). The house was brutally "updated" in the seventies: several of the original wood windows were crudely reconfigured and replaced with aluminum; a deck was tacked on to the west; and a master bedroom was hung vertiginously off the back, propped up on stilts, thirty feet above a creek.

The house was built on the carriage-house model, sited five feet from the road and pushed into the southeast corner of the lot. As a result, the small lot feels much larger, with sight lines extending from the street to the rear property line. This quality is exaggerated by the forest-like character of the lot, wooded by mature fir, cypress, and redwood trees. The site slopes steeply down from the road to the creek and back up, disappearing into a stand of trees, further increasing the sense of space.

What we liked about the house was the straightforward logic of its original plan and the quirky character of the site with its untapped potential. The architectural impulse that guided us in remodeling the house was to reinforce its urban-rural character by simultaneously reasserting its right-on-the-street quality and the feeling you get along the creek of being in a tree fort in a national forest. This project was completed in several stages, but the serious work was initiated rather abruptly when the Loma Prieta earthquake destroyed the brick chimney in 1989. At that time, a bedroom, bath, and study were added, as well as a variety of outdoor rooms: a forest lookout, sleeping deck, and campsite.

The solution to unlocking the site was a three-story, three-room addition that visually and physically connects the existing piano nobile to the creek via a stair tower. The only grand space in the house, the stair tower functions as a gallery, light well, and thermal chimney.

The entry stair was reconfigured as a straight line from the street, as it had been originally in the 1950s. At the top of the stair, we added a partially enclosed entry porch that functions as an urban mudroom, supported by a pair of angled timbers.

In the northwest corner of the original upper level, an under-utilized deck was replaced by an enclosed, tree-fort-like look-out supported on an unpeeled-redwood-log column. Similar to the entry porch, this room has stained Douglas fir framing exposed and set off against cladding of redwood board-on-board siding. A steel-framed sleeping deck, which is suspended underneath the look-out and clipped to the redwood-log column, overlooks the creek. Access from the master bedroom to the sleeping deck is through a sliding wall that has resin-coated plywood on the interior, redwood siding on the exterior. This wall slips out from the house and hangs from its track among the trees. The bed itself is mobile and rolls out onto the sleeping porch, filling it. At grade, the redwood column engages the existing trees at close hand and marks the path from the stair tower into the landscape. On the bottom story, partially cut into the hill, the study directly overlooks the creek.

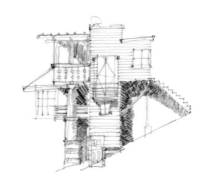

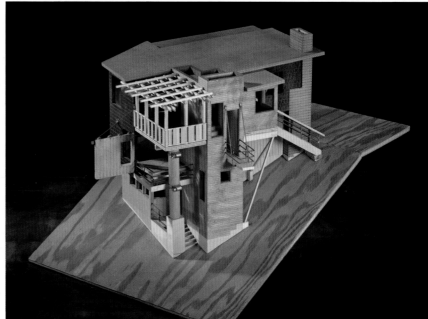

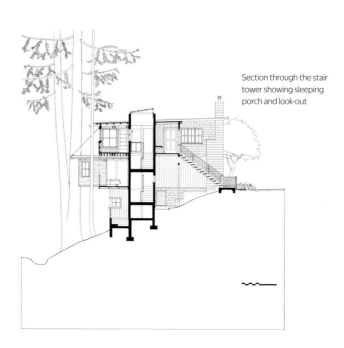

Section through the stair tower showing sleeping porch and look-out

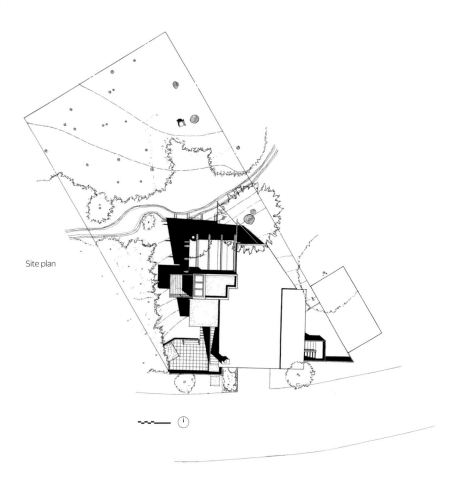

Site plan

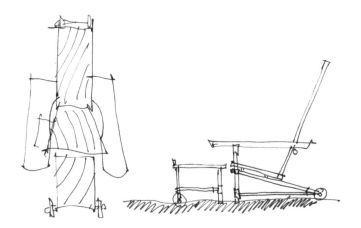

Sketches and prototype of the O.E. chair designed for the house.

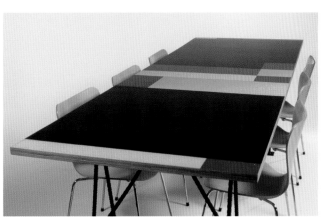

The "leftover table" can be expanded with leaves of various sizes, assembled from scraps salvaged from casework made for the house.

The Sonoma County site of this house slopes steeply to the southwest and overlooks the vineyards of the Valley of the Moon, where the sun can be brilliant, even harsh. Dry waxwood brush covers the site and there are several small California live oak trees along the upper edge. The primary view is to the south, both down into and out across the valley to the hills; there are less interesting but protected natural views to the east.

The owners of the house, a German couple, were captivated by California's wine country. Though committed modernists, our clients nonetheless wanted a house that was rooted to the particulars of its site. To this end, the house takes inspiration from the situated works of early northern European modern architecture even as it digresses from the dominant discourse of modernism to find connection with its surroundings.

The program called for a house for two, but with room to accommodate the family and friends who visit regularly. Privacy was a key issue, both inside and outside the house. To shield the house from views from the road and adjacent buildings, a wall slices through the site, running against the slope. This wall serves as a spine for the building, organizing circulation and structures in a series of alternating indoor and outdoor rooms that step up the hill. Each outdoor room has a character determined by its degree of architectural definition, the amount of sun protection it provides, and the type of planting it holds. At the bottom of the site is a sunny court with native planting and a lone California live oak; at the top is a shady moss garden. Between the two is an Innenhof, an outdoor room for living and dining. Bracketing this progression of rooms are a garden pavilion at the top of the site and a carport at the bottom.

Two towers punctuate the scheme. Containing a bedroom, a study, and an observation-sleeping platform, the taller tower forms an entry gate through which the primary circulation threads. The smaller tower serves as a guesthouse. Located for maximum views, privacy, and breezes, it sits on the wall, among trees, in the shady philosopher's garden at the highest point of the site. Communal living spaces surround the Innenhof. The loft-like master bedroom is perched above the living room and enclosed by shoji screens. A two-story bookcase that scales the east wall and makes an appearance in the bedroom above was improvised a couple of years after the house was finished. Tucked under the bedroom is the living room hearth. Although the hearth is the symbolic core of the house, the inhabitants inevitably gravitate from room to room, indoors and out, as the sun moves across the site. A combination of fixed metal sunshades, operable awnings, and wooden trellises keep the bright light at bay.

Von Stein House
Sonoma County, California, 1990–1993

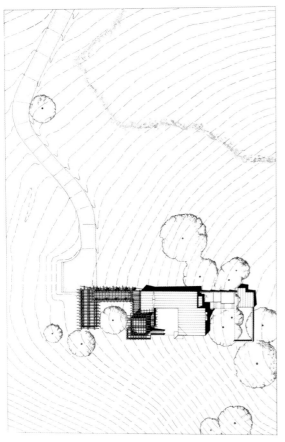

Site plan

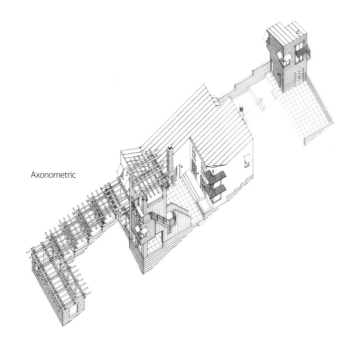

Axonometric

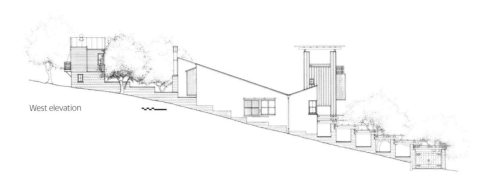

West elevation

Shaded courtyard in
Greece

Sensibility travels. Having gained a reputation for contextually and environmentally grounded architecture in California, we were anxious to test our circumstantial approach in diverse locations and climates. The Laybourne House and Art Barn was our first opportunity.

The property is on a mesa in Colorado that is ringed by isolated mountain peaks: from a third story there are views in every direction, and there is always a storm to watch. The site runs along a desolate, unprotected rim of a canyon that marks the transition from the Rockies to high desert. Forested by stands of pine, scrub oak, and sage, the mesa is punctuated by the contorted lines of blackened trees exploded by lightning.

When we met with our clients (who would fly out from New York) in Colorado during the programming and early design phases, we would go on architectural field trips, visiting contemporary and vernacular buildings to better understand the climate and how to live with it. The design of the house and art studio (in part an improvisation on the vernacular of Colorado's mining compounds) grew out of those visits. We admired the local precedents not for their imagery but for their straightforward approach to problem solving, particularly the strategies of siting, connection, and assembly. As architecture of expediency, the best mining compounds have much to teach us about creating habitable space in a hostile environment: familiar forms are reinvented, carved up, and reconnected in surprising ways, rendering them awkward and new through a fearlessly purposeful proto-modern sensibility.

Similar to the mining compounds, our design is composed of a number of buildings that are divided into places to sleep, retreat, and gather. The individual buildings are intended to both increase a sense of independence and privacy for family and friends, and multiply the possibilities for socializing. The division of the program into different buildings further allowed us to explore the particularities of the site's mountain location: the geology and topography, views and climate, and building and material traditions.

The compound spans two knolls, one hundred yards apart, that are high points on a canyon wall above the San Miguel River. The main house encloses one knoll, and the Art Barn is grafted on the side of a neighboring outcropping, hiking out over the canyon wall to command a view of neighboring mountain ranges. The Art Barn, also known as the Badger, was the first building to be completed and is used both for special projects and occasionally as a guesthouse. During design and construction it was our headquarters. In the swale between the knolls, a tent camp for guests rings an open fire pit. The main house is divided into two halves: the lodge and the cookhouse; each has sleeping accommodations. The master bedroom is a separate structure. These elements wrap an outdoor room that is animated by an exterior hearth/barbecue, the heart of the encampment year-round.

During the programming phase, we learned of the clients' strong desire to be continually reminded of where they were by experiencing the smells, temperature, seasons, and landscape of the place. We designed the house so that people moving through it are visually aligned and realigned with near and distant features of the numerous surrounding peaks. Circulation between the main structures is covered but open to the weather. The master bed is mounted on tracks so it can be rolled out to a trestle that extends to the edge of the canyon.

Laybourne House and Art Barn
Telluride, Colorado, 1991–1993

Ophir Mine in Colorado

Telluride mine in Colorado

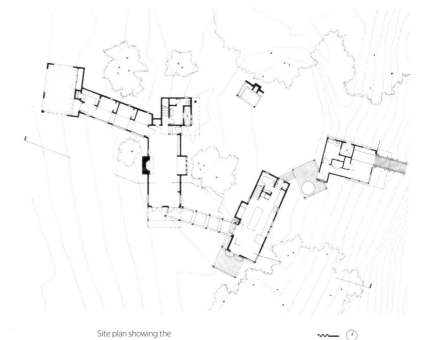

Site plan showing the
ground floor

Site plan

Section through the knoll
showing central outdoor
dining room

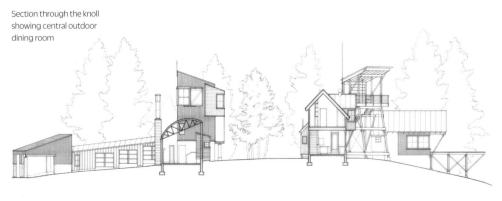

Overflow guests can
be accommodated in
Pullman beds

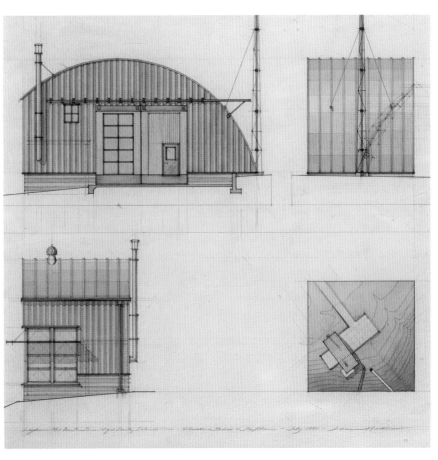

Art Barn elevations

Newport Beach House
Newport Beach, California, 1994–1997

When the summer house was originally built, Newport Beach was a quiet strip of Southern California shoreline. Today, the little seaside cottages contemporary with our clients' house are mostly gone, and the Balboa Peninsula is now packed with house after house, each stretching from side to side to achieve maximum lot coverage. "South of somewhere" architectural aspirations prevail and a desire to maximize the view of the sea is a collectively shared idée fixe. Outdoor living is limited to barbequing and sun bathing on narrow decks. Walking, Rollerblading, or bicycling along the boardwalk that runs behind the houses is a common part of the locals' daily routine; looking into the houses is as popular as looking out to the sea.

One of the few small houses that remained from the forties, the Newport Beach House renovation was commissioned by our Northern California clients. They had been generously sharing their house with family and friends for some time. Our clients — avid surfers with three young children — asked us to remodel the house for year-round weekend use.

Halfway through the initial design process, the lot next door came up for sale. This presented the tantalizing possibility of a rare interruption of the continuous densification of the beachfront fabric. Our clients were fond of the gable-roofed, shingled (somewhat frumpy) understatement of the existing house more like the casual Northern California surroundings of their primary home. They wanted to add minimal square footage to the new lot and focus primary attention on outdoor living. The programmatic requirements were simple: to provide flexible sleeping quarters for spontaneous sleepovers; to have one main living space indoors; to put almost everything else outdoors (spaces for cooking, eating, showering, and bathing); and to make it all very clear and easy to use for both old and new guests.

We were sympathetic to the idea of retaining the character of the original house and wanted both house and garden to allow for the contemporary and playful expression of the interests of this young family and their friends. We also wanted to develop the garden as a series of outdoor rooms specific to these activities and yet able to accommodate the unexpected.

The house remodel began with the surgical removal of a previously added garage and the addition of a new gable perpendicular to the original one — with garage below and bunkroom and baths above. We then made a series of adaptations to these two basic gables: lifting roofs to catch views and to let in light. We located a small guest room, half bath, and "surf shack" on the north (street) side of the lot, shielding the garden from the street. In turn, the garden screens the guest room, half bath, and "surf shack" from the boardwalk. Finally, a series of outdoor rooms were defined by a mixture of lightweight structures (a trellised carport, a trellised dining area, a vine-enclosed hot tub, an outdoor shower, and a roofed cooking counter with barbecue) and dense vegetation (including ginger, bird-of-paradise, bamboo, jasmine, and grass).

The exterior materials loosely record the additions and adaptations to the original (reshingled) cedar structure, resulting in a collage of redwood board and batten and horizontal siding, cedar shingle, and copper roofs. All the wood was oiled and left to weather. The windows and doors were painted with Richard Diebenkorn's *Ocean Park* palette of blues and greens and the occasional yellow. In contrast to the dark and unobtrusive exterior, the interior is mainly white, with color coming from the fir floors, vivid carpets, and terrazzo countertops. No written instructions are necessary for guests. And sixteen can sleep in a pinch.

For the many passers-by on the boardwalk, the garden has become a kind of parklike gift: a lush gap between the cheek-by-jowl neighbors, with their outward-focused insistence. From within the garden, where most of a typical day is spent, various levels of privacy are possible, from the "see and be seen" outer layer to the seclusion of the bathing area and guest room. On a hot night in summer, indulgence in the myth of subtropical California is possible. On a stormy day in winter, the house feels hunkered down — shingles graying, redwood blackening, and copper turning green.

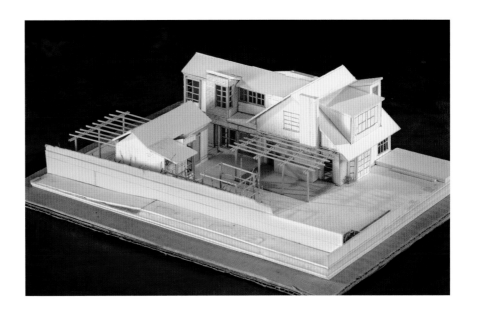

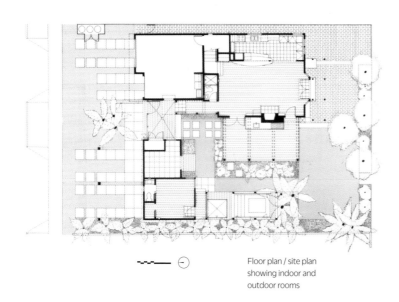

Floor plan / site plan
showing indoor and
outdoor rooms

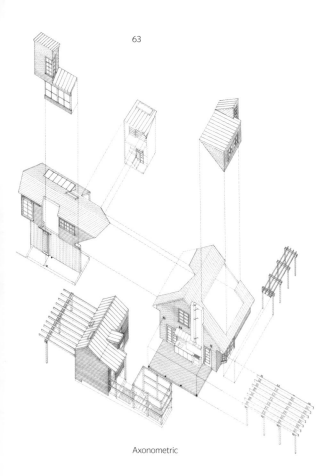

Axonometric

The cardinal rule of improvisation is not to say no to a pass or suggestion. Transform or reinvent but don't reject: negation is a dead end. On the way to the airport after our first site visit, in a theatrical gesture, one the clients, a film director, insisted we take an unplanned detour back through the small fishing village of Menemsha on Martha's Vineyard. It was raining and we were cutting it close. Double-parked, she rushed to the center of a dense warren of fishing shacks. Arms out, she declared that it was none of the buildings but "the space between," the scale, that captured her sense of the island architecture. When we later presented our schematic design options, we included one that took our visit to Menemsha as its departure. They picked it.

The MV House sits on a gently sloping, sparsely vegetated site in Chilmark, a rural town on Martha's Vineyard. Views downhill to the east are of fields defined by stone walls that extend down to Nashaquitsa Pond. In the distance, to the north at the mouth of the pond, is Menemsha, made famous by the movie *Jaws*. At the southern end of the pond is a small harbor, with a glimpse of the Atlantic beyond. Our clients have a long history on the island. They remember uninterrupted vistas, which have been altered in recent years by the construction of neighboring houses. One of their requests was that we attempt to edit views in siting the house, reclaiming their memory of the unobstructed landscape.

While we found the architecture of Menemsha mesmerizing, with its tiny gable-roofed structures, sliced and diced, endlessly modified by additions and subtractions, we agreed with our clients' assessment: the houses

MV House
Martha's Vineyard, Massachusetts, 1995–1998

and boat sheds were not what made the village visually compelling. Within the dense confluence of buildings and boats, complex geometries played with scale, creating forced perspectives and framing unexpected views. In the pockets between buildings, the architecture became curiously distorted (in part because you couldn't get back far enough to apprehend the whole), and the traditional quality of the elements was eclipsed by the strange, ultramodern sense of fragmented and compressed space. However, individual structures, when you looked closely, expressed tradition and innovation in equal measure. This tension between the formulaic and the improvisational gives the local vernacular a collage-like quality. In this context, the local planning requirements (heavily weighted toward gable-roofed structures) didn't inhibit our creativity.

Working with this notion of collage, we divided the house into three parts (one for parents, one for children, and one for everyone) and expressed each part as an independent gabled "shed." Each of the sheds was sited independently, factoring in breezes, views, and

other environmental criteria. The three pieces come together at various angles, like boats casually docked at a pier, and share a common deck. Circulation between them is on the exterior. The space between the three structures, which would be an exterior courtyard in one of our West Coast projects, is roofed over and screened in. An outdoor room adapted for the island climate, this screened porch — which features a fireplace, dining table, and crisscross circulation — functions like a central courtyard. It is the most significant social space of the house. The juxtaposition of the three buildings not only creates provocative spaces for reading or art projects, it also helps frame and edit near and distant views.

The division of the house into separate sheds breaks down the scale of the architecture, making it fit comfortably into the neighborhood, especially from the water. Materials were chosen to help the residence recede into the surrounding landscape: cedar shingles and siding, copper shingles and standing seam roofs, mahogany decking, painted steel, and sailcloth.

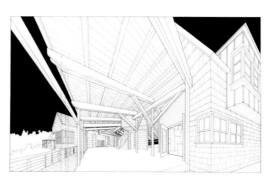

Perspective of the screened porch

weather
Raof

Heated

Menemsha, Martha's Vineyard

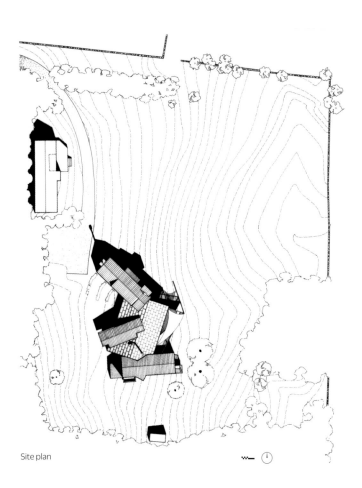

Site plan

Exploded axonometric
showing the three sheds and
central screened porch

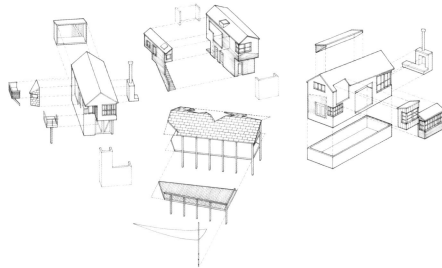

Located in the Eastern Panhandle of West Virginia, this house sits on a swath of land that encompasses a tree-lined rural road, an open meadow, and a dense, third-growth deciduous forest where a south-facing promontory commands views of the Potomac River. In winter the site has stark views to Civil War battlefields on distant ridges. In summer it is lush and mercilessly humid, with the river nearly obscured by dense undergrowth.

The house is designed to serve as the owner's primary residence, as well as a rural retreat for visiting family and friends, and a gathering place for colleagues from Washington D.C. and New York. Because the owner wanted to experience the site, the river, and views of the distant landscape as immediately as possible, careful placement of the house on the site was crucial. The approach to the house runs along the edge of the narrow meadow, culminating in a central courtyard carved out of the dense forest. Two stone walls reach out like arms to embrace the courtyard. Between the two "arms," a single-story gallery links three main buildings—the garage, guest quarters, and owner's residence— and orients each to views into the forest and down across the river.

The three main buildings are simple shed-roofed structures, conceptually remodeled to accommodate demands of climate, light, views, and program. Exterior corridors cut through the undergrowth in front of each, extending interior views down to the river. Complementing this horizontal engagement with the site is a four-story tower rising beside the library and living area. With an open porch, screened sleeping deck, enclosed study, and lookout, the tower offers elevated views of the immediate site and distant ridges beyond the river.

In addition to responding to its surrounding landscape, the building also responds to its context by drawing on local building traditions, materials, craftsmanship, and practice. Local masons built the limestone "arms" with native stone, and local timber framers used state-grown oak to craft the timber-framed structures (straightforwardly augmented with steel braces where necessary). Floors and casework are of eastern cherry, and a combination of metal and wood siding reflects and interprets indigenous building practice. Colors drawn from the autumn palette of the site sustain the building's warmth in the bleak winter months and help it recede into the surrounding landscape in late spring, summer, and fall.

Potomac Retreat
Eastern Panhandle, West Virginia, 1996–1998

Sheperdstown,
West Virginia

Railroad tower in
Thurmond, West Virginia

Floor plan / site plan showing
indoor and outdoor rooms,
with second floor plan above

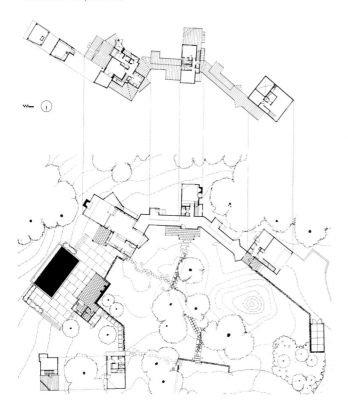

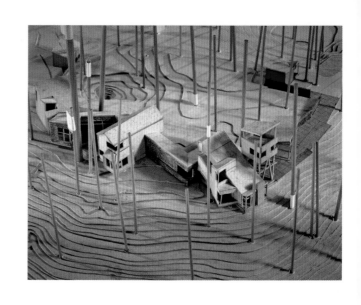

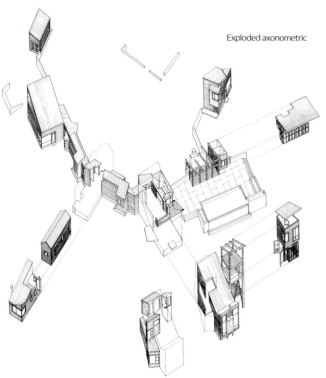

Exploded axonometric

Local barn in transit,
Bozeman, Montana

Avis Ranch

Park County, Montana, 1996–2003

This long-term project was haunted by a question initially spoken out of frustration and in jest: what would a farmer do? The question was posed by our clients, who hired us to design a sustainable home and headquarters for their Montana cattle ranch. The property was assembled piecemeal, resulting in a 17,000-acre ranch that proved to be as complex as it was spectacular. Spanning three drainages with active creeks, it hosts numerous ecosystems, ranging from high desert to coniferous forest. Consequently, the choice of a site for a new homestead was not obvious. Cut through with contradictions, the program was pulled between the clients' desires to have a view, get away, run an efficient operation, and be good stewards of the land. After a year of traversing the property, consulting with neighbors, and studying the environment, a half-dozen sites recommended themselves, most in the far expanses of the ranch, but something about building anew wasn't quite making sense to either the client or to us.

A farmer would build near the road. He already had. Clustered near the road in two compounds were the remains of the original homestead and ranch buildings. The rural road could provide easy access to the buildings in winter and a sense of transparency that would smooth the family's transition into the surrounding community. As the land was already disturbed and the infrastructure was intact, our ecological footprint could be minimal. Although this strategy was at odds with a number of our clients' initial requests, the environmental logic was compelling. And as architects, we sublimated our formal ambitions in order to integrate the new program with the existing buildings. Between the various structures, we were able to satisfy our clients, while significantly reducing the scope and scale of the project. Our green ambitions became an act of reclamation: one part renovation, one part adaptive reuse, one part infill.

Montana is deeply divided over development issues. The state attracts and needs people but mourns the loss of its rural character and the aggressive architectural intrusions into its fragile and often pristine landscape. Historic rural buildings disappear frequently, as they are seldom maintained and rarely renovated. When they are, they are frequently sold and reappear as historicized tourist attractions. It is against this backdrop that we sought to explore alternative development models that sidestep the state's typical preservation formulas.

The original ranch consisted of two clusters of buildings on an unimproved country road outside Clyde Park, a sparsely populated rural town in south central Montana. In the two clusters, a total of five buildings were renovated, two new utility structures were added, and most recently an oversize cookhouse (see page 96) and equipment barn were built to accommodate larger gatherings. While the landscape conferred a kind of rural monumentality, the individual buildings were quite modest. When we began, the family homestead had been virtually abandoned for more than fifty years, adding to the sterility of the landscape. All the buildings had been given over to housing the livestock. Over the almost twenty-year course of this project, we resited or restored, to varying degrees, all of the original buildings within the two compounds.

Our philosophy toward renovation was unsentimental; our goal was not historic preservation as much as the preservation of rural life, which entails continued adaptation to changing conditions. With this in mind, our program included more nuanced alterations, from modest fence realignments to the more audacious reorientation of a creek to its natural drainage. Architecturally, our intention was to demonstrate that the discarded structures could have a utility beyond being part of the historical record. We wanted to explore an unromantic attitude toward the historic structures that retained their integrity while addressing a contemporary sensibility. To that end, we chose to express what was new as new, while maintaining what was old as blatantly so.

The family homestead was the first to be completed. It is made up of three buildings: a renovated farmhouse (most recently used as a barn); a defunct granary, which we redesigned as a bunkhouse and gym for winter recreation; and a new car barn, fabricated out of 2x lumber sistered to create columns and beams. The ranch headquarters, one mile down the road, is composed of six buildings and a round pen. Unlike the family homestead, the headquarters had been in use in some way for over a hundred years, although a number of its buildings were in a state of near collapse. To return the headquarters to full functionality, we converted a small two-cell granary into an office and guest quarters, and reconstructed the outhouse into a composting toilet, even refurbishing the old "three-holer" toilet seat as a light fixture. Lastly, a new hay barn replaced an existing steel Quonset.

Ultimately, it was a farmer's pragmatism that led to the success of the project, not only as an architectural entity but also as a functional piece of the community. As a model for rural development, our approach was greatly appreciated by many Clyde Park residents, fulfilling our collective desire to make a positive connection with the community.

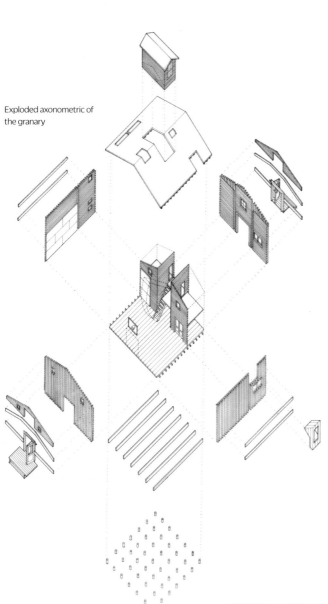

Exploded axonometric of
the granary

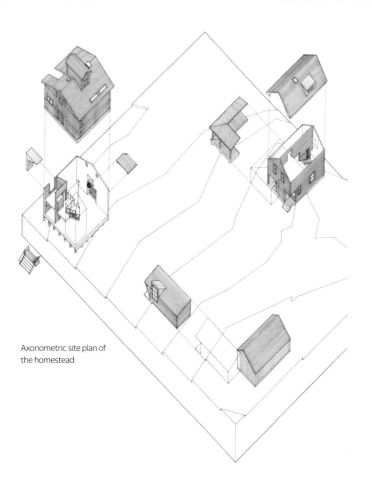

Axonometric site plan of
the homestead

Homestead and granary
before renovation (ready
to roll)

Wilsal, Montana

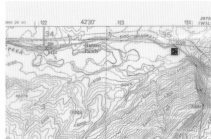

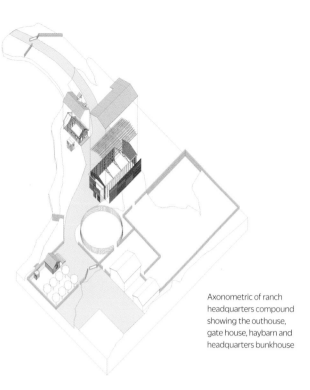

Axonometric of ranch
headquarters compound
showing the outhouse,
gate house, haybarn and
headquarters bunkhouse

Ranch headquarters under
construction

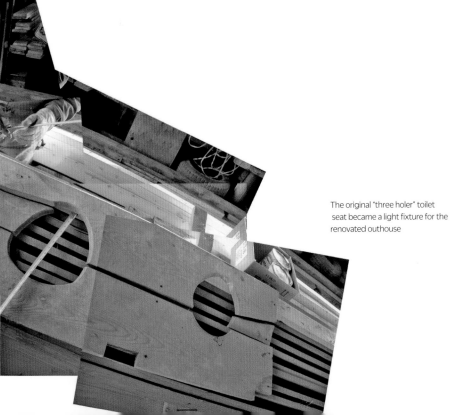

The original "three holer" toilet seat became a light fixture for the renovated outhouse

We had been working on the Avis Ranch for nearly twenty years when we started to design the Cookhouse. The additions and renovations we had already done to the historic homestead were well received locally and by the profession, so we were nervous about adding a new piece. We were concerned that the significantly larger scale of the new structure would compete with the Granary, which was the centerpiece of the Montana compound, a landmark visible for miles as one descends into the Brackett Creek valley. Our goal, therefore, was to build modestly and with minimal impact on the landscape of the existing ranch.

We started by deciding to site the Cookhouse on the south side of, and across a small creek from, the Granary. The creek— which had become little more than a drainage ditch—was restored and replanted with willows, dogwood, and other native riparian vegetation to provide a degree of separation from the agricultural compound and road beyond. The Equipment Barn is located adjacent to the previously rehabilitated Granary and connects to the Cookhouse by a footbridge over the creek. We adopted a one-and-a-half-story, broad-eaved, gable-roofed structure similar to local hay barns for the Cookhouse to bring down its scale and allow the two-and-a-half-story Granary to remain the anchor of the compound. The Equipment Barn is a low shed off to the side of the compound.

The Cookhouse's elongated east-west axis is not only optimal for solar gain, but also ideal for views. This orientation, moreover, presents the narrow face of the building to the most intense wind and weather. Its second story pushes out from underneath the roof in various ways to grab light, steal a view, or expel hot air. Both floors are organized in plan along a central circulation spine. This generous central hallway with a wood-burning stove links all interior spaces and functions not only as a gallery and social space, but also as a massive air duct connecting the entire house to the thermal chimney. The thermal chimney punctures the roof at its ridge and keeps the house cool, even in the extreme heat of summer, making air-conditioning unnecessary. In cold months, the house is heated with a ground-source heat pump and energy-efficient wood stoves. The low ceiling and thermal chimney help maximize thermal performance. The gable roof's substantial overhang and wraparound porch provide ample options for working and relaxing outside, protected from the wind, rain, snow, and sun.

Cookhouse
Park County, Montana, 2008–2012

Wilsal, Montana

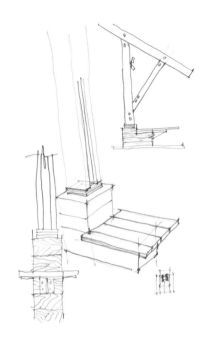

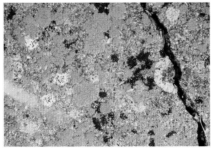

Materials palette

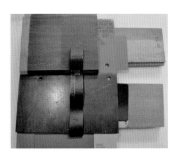

Serious Play
Thomas Fisher

"The struggle of maturity is to recover the seriousness of the child at play."
Friedrich Nietszche

The playfulness of Richard Fernau and Laura Hartman's work remains one of its most striking features, and as such, it offers an energetic reinterpretation of the Bay Area tradition, an approach to architecture long associated with the San Francisco region. While that tradition has gone through at least three phases since its emergence in the 1880s, it has had a continuous evolution, with buildings characterized by informal, asymmetrical compositions; flexible and often meandering floor plans; an openness to the natural environment; and the frequent use of unpainted, natural materials.[1] The architects of Fernau + Hartman almost couldn't help but be influenced by that tradition, with their first office located behind a house by the early master of the movement, Bernard Maybeck, and close to Maybeck's own former home and studio.

But these architects have reimagined the Bay Area tradition in ways that give it new life and that set their work apart from that of colleagues who have turned that tradition into a formulaic aesthetic. They have embraced, instead, the improvisational nature, its environmental responsiveness, and its eccentric sense of humor, while also improving upon the sometimes-dark interiors and drab hues of the tradition. Although their buildings all differ in subtle ways in response to the particular program and site, all have certain qualities in common: colorful, collage-like combinations of materials; light-filled, climate-responsive spaces; and expressive and experientially rich forms. In this way, Fernau + Hartman shows how the Bay Area tradition represents not a style, but a sensibility: an open, inventive, playful approach to life.

That sensibility runs counter to the "seriousness" that we often associate with being adults, but Fernau + Hartman's work, like that of some of the most important artists and thinkers of the last century, suggests that only through playfulness will we ever find the solutions to the most serious problems of our time. The historian Johan Huizinga first elevated our understanding of the cultural importance of play, but he also reflected the bias of many adults in defining play as "not serious."[2] Fernau + Hartman has freed itself from that bias and shown, through its architecture, that the best design represents a serious form of play, open to what a situation or setting suggests in order to find the most appropriate response.

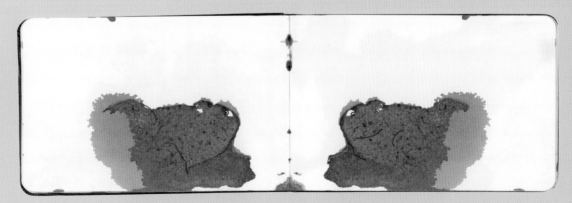

Richard Fernau
On the other hand
Tache drawing, 2003

We can all learn from the firm's example. "There's nothing easier to lose than playfulness," wrote the novelist Jim Harrison,[3] and our educational system, with its emphasis on discipline, and our economy, with its focus on efficiency, have both made the playfulness essential to creativity and innovation easy for us to lose. As another great novelist, Samuel Butler, once observed, "All animals, except man, know that the principal business of life is to enjoy it,"[4] and few architects remind us of that fact more Fernau + Hartman.

Too many architects over the last century have gone in the opposite direction, veering from a puritanical modernism to a sometimes-silly postmodernism and an often-inscrutable poststructuralism, leading to architecture's current schizophrenic state, split between austere simplicity and extravagant complexity. In that context, Fernau + Hartman's work comes as a welcome relief. The firm has had the courage to walk away from the somberness of high-style architecture to embrace the tradition of wry humor found in the work of modern artists like Robert Rauschenberg and John Cage and the sense of ad hoc invention found in vernacular architecture and improvisational theater. Richard Fernau captures that sensibility well when he observes that "alleys are always more interesting than Main Street."[5]

Look at the projects in this book as a kind of architectural wordplay on the word "play." Sometimes, as in Fernau + Hartman's Anderson/Ayers House (see page 118), the playfulness of the architecture expresses a program literally intended for the staging of plays. Designed for a dramatist and writer and their child, the house has a central area that steps down like a theater to a stagelike space at the bottom, ideal for accommodating visiting performers. In other projects, like the design for the Avis Ranch in Montana (see page 84), Fernau + Hartman has used play more as a metaphor for the character and arrangement of buildings. Sitting in a spectacular landscape surrounded by mountains, the ranch's idiosyncratic wooden structures look like the weather-beaten characters in a Western, standing about as if waiting for a shoot-out to occur.

Other houses by the firm have similar theatrical effects. The Mann House (see page 126) connects its public and private spaces with stairs from the bedrooms that dramatically descend from either direction to the main living area, while the artist owners have separate "backstage" studios in which to work. The Potomac Retreat (see page 76) offers another version of this idea. Designed for a former governor and able to accommodate visiting friends and colleagues, the house forms a kind of amphitheater, with a series of structures that seem to jostle and joust with each other as if performing on some sort of political stage.

The playfulness of Fernau + Hartman's work seems to attract clients who value that quality in their own lives. In the MV House (see page 66), the architects have arranged three gable-roofed structures around a large, central screened porch in which family members can gather and engage in physical activity with a freedom not always possible in furnished rooms. In the urban homestead dubbed the "Bucket of Blood" (see page 136), a high-ceilinged central space has enough room to let the owners play sports like basketball and boxing.

Playing off our ideas about the past also characterizes a lot of Fernau + Hartman's architecture. The Laybourne House and Art Barn (see page 48) riff on the image we all have of mining camps in the mountains, with a series of gable-, shed-, and Quonset-roofed structures that recall the improvisational way in which those compounds often evolved. And in a direct reference to the lives of miners, the architects have placed a bed on

Straw-bale House wall detail and section

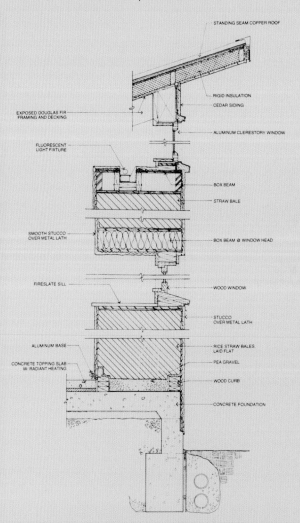

STANDING SEAM COPPER ROOF

RIGID INSULATION

CEDAR SIDING

EXPOSED DOUGLAS FIR FRAMING AND DECKING

ALUMINUM CLERESTORY WINDOW

FLUORESCENT LIGHT FIXTURE

BOX BEAM

STRAW BALE

SMOOTH STUCCO OVER METAL LATH

BOX BEAM @ WINDOW HEAD

FIRESLATE SILL

WOOD WINDOW

STUCCO OVER METAL LATH

ALUMINUM BASE

RICE STRAW BALES, LAID FLAT

CONCRETE TOPPING SLAB W/ RADIANT HEATING

PEA GRAVEL

WOOD CURB

CONCRETE FOUNDATION

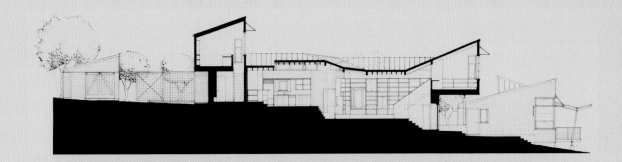

rails, enabling it to move outdoors on a trestle, like the cars that used to carry precious material out of the mines.

The Berggruen House (see page 24), with its metal-clad, shack-like extensions to a central cookhouse, recalls the migrant farmworker housing that used to occupy the site in the midst of Napa's vineyards, reimagining a type of dwelling too often overlooked as architecture. The additions at the Barnacle House (see page 172) and the renovation of the "Big House" at the compound in Nonquitt (see page 142) offer variations on that theme. Both projects involved the grafting of new structures onto distinguished older houses, recalling the tradition of adding lean-to sheds and projecting porches onto buildings. By cladding these additions in diverse materials and treating them as if they had been built over a long period of time, Fernau + Hartman reminds us of a more frugal past in which people mainly used the materials immediately available to them and built only when they had the money to do so.

A sense of embracing thrift also comes through in projects like the Straw-bale House (1995–1999). There, Fernau + Hartman captured vernacular strategies not just in the form of the building, but also in its construction, using straw-bale walls to create thermal mass as well as glass walls to open out to the views. Parsimony of a different sort occurs in the Fernau/Cunniff House (see page 32). Starting with a tiny house and garage, the architects added a three-story addition off the back without greatly adding to the building's footprint, using the site's steep slope and Berkeley's mild climate to great effect, with balconies expanding the living

and sleeping areas while preserving the heavily wooded lot. A variety of wood-siding types not only distinguishes the additions from the original structure, but also recalls the consistent inconsistency of vernacular builders, using what they had at hand.

Fernau + Hartman's narrative inventiveness has a programmatic role to play as well. In the Cheesecake Cohousing Consortium (see page 110), for instance, the variety of cladding materials—painted plywood, stained cedar, corrugated metal—define different levels of public and private spaces for the seven households sharing this one building. At the same time, the use of covered outdoor spaces and of tent platforms for both residents and visitors gives this community a lot to play with and a lot of play (meaning flexibility) in how it grows and changes. Fernau + Hartman's strategic, loose-fit approach to architecture provides the ideal match for such a complicated program. The firm is as responsive to human ecosystems as to natural ones.

This improvisational approach also works well on complicated sites. The Snell/Sanders House (see page 152), for example, occupies a steep slope in a highly visible location, and the architects have embraced those constraints with a wedge-like structure off of which angled indoor and outdoor spaces step up or down as necessary to accommodate the terrain changes. The house's paint colors also match those of the soil and the sky to help it visually disappear in the landscape. Fernau + Hartman's buildings do not mimic the forms of nature but instead adapt to it in ways that seem unforced and almost inevitable, which sets their work apart from other sustainability-minded architects, who too often try too hard to make their buildings seem "natural."

The design, construction, and inhabitation of a building brings with it a sense of accomplishment and vicarious enjoyment not unlike that which comes from participating in or experiencing others play. While we rarely think of architecture in these terms, the built environment sets the stage of our lives and makes us all actors in the comedies and dramas of living. And very few architecture firms pursue that idea as directly and express it as thoroughly as Fernau + Hartman. The firm's work continually surprises and delights the inhabitants as they move around and through it, because it not only plays with the elements of architecture—form and space, material and color—but also with the expectations of architecture. "Play always has a sacred place . . . in which it happens,"[6] observed the writer Diane Ackerman, and Fernau + Hartman has shown us just how playful the sacred place of play can be.

1. Lewis Mumford, "The Architecture of the Bay Region," in *Domestic Architecture of the San Francisco Bay Region* (San Francisco: San Francisco Museum of Art, 1949).
2. Johan Huizinga, *Homo Ludens: A Study of the Play-Element in Culture* (Boston: Beacon Press, 1955), 13.
3. Jim Harrison, *True North* (New York: Grove Press, 2004), 196.
4. Samuel Butler, *The Way of All Flesh* (London: Penguin Books, 1947), chapter 19.
5. That comment also represents a playful response to the question that Robert Venturi asks at the end of his manifesto *Complexity and Contradiction in Architecture*, "Is not Main Street almost all right?"
6. Diane Ackerman, *Deep Play* (New York: Vintage Books, 1999), 6.

Site layout with Cheesecake members

Crazy quilt, Montana

Cheesecake Cohousing Consortium
Northern California, 1990–1993

This project was an experiment in retirement housing, design process, and, ultimately, aesthetics. Our involvement began when we were hired by a group of seven couples to plan a communal living compound on a river in Northern California. The core group had bonded several years earlier when their children were in preschool and had remained friends ever since. At a certain point, they decided to buy land with the thought of vacationing and ultimately retiring together. Like with cohousing experiments for young families, the idea was to design a residential community where a number of people could live independently but provide mutual support and share facilities such as a kitchen and laundry.

They made decisions by consensus, which at first seemed like it might be difficult for us to follow, but proved to be the contrary. We presented alternatives to the group and discussed options; however, we were not included in the final deliberations. Instead, we would receive a written critique of our designs that expressly excluded any design solutions and only addressed points of agreement and concern, the resolution of which was left to us. Although somewhat ponderous at first, this method proved to be an effective means of collaborating with a complex group.

For everyone to be able to afford to buy in, the compound needed to be quite economical. To avoid financial casualties, a monetary "allotment" was set for a basic dwelling unit, which could be augmented (within limits) as individual requirements and resources dictated. At the end of the design phase, the wish list of wants and desires exceeded the established budget. To clarify the decisions that needed to be considered, we presented a color-coded model of the compound: green for the budgeted programs (communal kitchen and basic accommodations); yellow for supplemental amenities (library and laundry); red for individual requests (extra room, dormers, bay windows, etc.). To our surprise, the group approved all the supplemental additions and adopted our diagrammatic color-coding as the color scheme.

For economy's sake, the largest exterior volumes are clad in plywood, and to protect from potential flooding, the buildings are lifted five feet off the forest floor. Simple concrete Sonotube footings support glulam beams on which the plywood volumes sit. The additions are supported by 4x4 posts, while adjacent shared verandas are raised and articulated with 2x4 knee-braced Douglas fir posts milled from the few trees cut on-site. The buildings are designed to grow old with the group, incorporating short-term low-cost and space-saving strategies, midterm adaptability strategies, and long-term phasing and expansion strategies. Circulation spaces (including a future elevator and ramps), common rooms, and the individualized programmatic requirements of each of the seven private quarters modify the three basic sheds that anticipate change over time.

A generation later, families have grown, the river has flooded, and Cheesecake continues to come through high and dry.

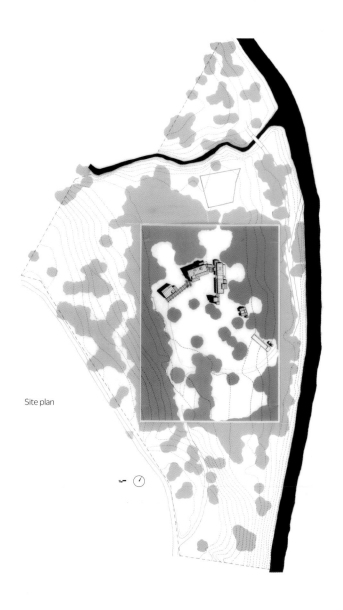

Site plan

Ponte Vecchio, Florence

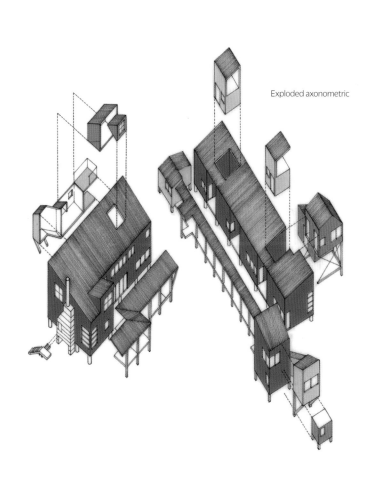

Exploded axonometric

Picasso
Mandolin and Clarinet
1913

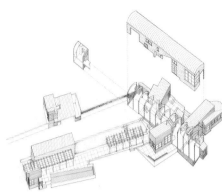

Exploded axonometric

Anderson/Ayers House
Marin County, California, 1994–1999

The vernacular agricultural buildings of Marin County in Northern California, particularly barrel-vaulted barns and improvisational poultry sheds, were, in part, the inspiration for the Anderson/Ayers House. The site is in the hills of west Marin, where the land slopes steeply toward the west and overlooks a reservoir, with farmlands and the Pacific Ocean beyond. Although often sunny, the coastal microclimate is subject to intense breezes and chilling fogs that can become uncomfortable in fall and winter. Periodically, the rain is very heavy.

The house is a second home for a dramatist, a writer, and their young child. With the exception of two studios and a pool, their program was fairly typical for a family of this size. However, this seemingly simple project was made more complex by their desire for a house that would be introverted on the exterior and extroverted in the interior—a "barn/theater" that not only provides a retreat from the wind and fog, but also serves as a venue for traveling players.

Because the site is exposed and potentially visible from a distance, we adapted two primary siting strategies: first, to straddle a wind-blown, tree-covered rock outcropping and second, to dig the house into the hill. The discovery of an underground spring caused the original parti to be stretched out and inspired us to design a "circumstantial water feature" in the newly opened gap between the structures. In the final design, we divided the house into two wings: one comprising the writing studio, pool, and pool house; and the other being the main living space.

That living area is a barrel-vaulted "bar" that is situated across the slope and is oriented more or less east-west, with its narrow face turned to the wind. At one end, the house disappears into the grade, and at the other, it gestures out, affording a view over the wind-dwarfed oaks to the reservoir below. The bar is stepped along its length, naturally creating the slope of a theater, establishing the central common space as the "stage," with the kitchen and master bedroom occupying stage left and stage right, respectively. The barrel-roof piece is the structure—or the chart, as it is called in jazz—around which the other elements improvise. Like riffs, these secondary pieces modify and reinterpret the whole. Architecturally, they create contrasting "stage sets" on the interior and sheltered rooms on the exterior.

Rendering of the house, showing unbuilt bunkhouse

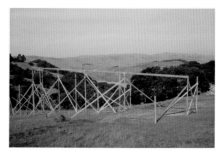

Story poles on the site

Marin County hills

Faial, Azores

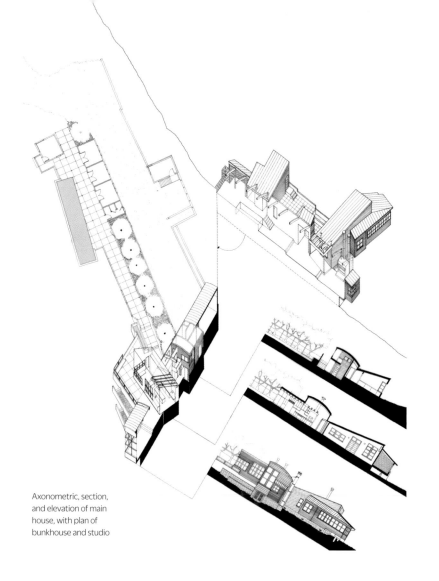

Axonometric, section, and elevation of main house, with plan of bunkhouse and studio

Situated on a ridge in California's Sonoma County, this residence has a 360-degree view of the surrounding vineyards. In the distance, to the west, is the fog-smothered inner coastal range. The view is mesmerizing. Building there wasn't our first choice; it wasn't even our second. Panoramic views have a way of neutralizing the landscape, rendering it banal. For aesthetic reasons, we would have slid the house just off the ridge, out of sight from other properties; for practical reasons, we would have tucked it into the landscape out of the wind and oriented it for sun. Ironically, we were confined to the most visible location, a flattened pad on the ridge, which was defined as the building envelope by the developer and enforced by the county. Although there were no immediate neighbors, the site was visible at a distance from other houses perched on adjacent hills, making the site feel oddly exposed. To begin to address these givens, we pulled the pieces of the program apart to create a compound like the modest agricultural villas that punctuate the hills in Tuscany. The pieces of the compound could then be used to define a protected interior courtyard out of the wind, with framed views of the surrounding countryside.

The program was for a family of three: a couple and their teenage son. At the time they commissioned us, the clients lived in Arquitectonica's rationalist Pink House in Miami. The iconic vibrant-hued house is a disciplined "bar" in plan: an attenuated rectangle with similarly proportioned rooms lined up along a straight corridor. Although completely different from the house we ultimately designed, the Pink House served as an important touchstone for our discussions. It revealed the depth of the Manns' interest in and understanding of architecture. It also underscored their love of color.

While the Manns' rationalist experiment had taught them that spaces need not be grand to be good, the spatial compression of the Pink House also taught them the value of modernist spatial flow, where functions and rooms can overlap. They knew that a house could be quite modest in size if the interior spaces were interconnected, one borrowing from another.

Of our designs, the Manns were particularly fond of the Von Stein House (see page 40), which they visited in the Valley of the Moon not far away. A long shed with a courtyard cut out, the Von Stein House parallels the line of a steep slope. Its site couldn't be more different from the Manns' narrow, shaved ridge in Dry Creek. However, what they especially liked about the Von Stein House was the courtyard, the dining-kitchen-living configuration, and the loftlike master bedroom. It's not unusual, when collaborating with clients on the design of a new house, to begin by conceptually "remodeling" the formal logic of another house of ours that they admire. The final results never resemble each other, because the sites and design circumstances are never the same.

The exercise was to improvise on the Von Stein House, to test whether it could be rearranged to work well in a new set of circumstances. Sometimes such efforts result in a rich variation; sometimes they are a dead end. In this case, it worked. We bent and folded the shed to form a butterfly and accommodate a bedroom at either end. The living, dining, and kitchen spaces are recomposed around a double-height central hall. The two stairways lead up from the hall to the separate wings: one containing the son's bedroom, the other comprising the master bedroom and an office that sits over the front door. In addition, the butterfly is crimped to begin to form an exterior courtyard. To further define the courtyard, we added two outbuildings. The principal outbuilding is a variation on a vernacular "dogtrot" plan: two rooms divided by a covered outdoor space. In this case, the outdoor space is shared by a painting studio and guest room. This building is also bent to enlarge the central courtyard. Finally, one end of the central court is bracketed by a utility building, which defines the entry. The juxtaposition of the two opposing chevrons made it possible to create a series of outdoor spaces to accommodate varying weather conditions.

Mann House
Sonoma County, California, 1998–2002

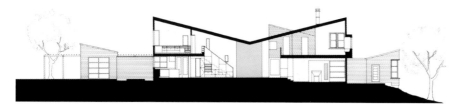

Section through the butterfly

Dog trot house in Northern California

Bodie, California

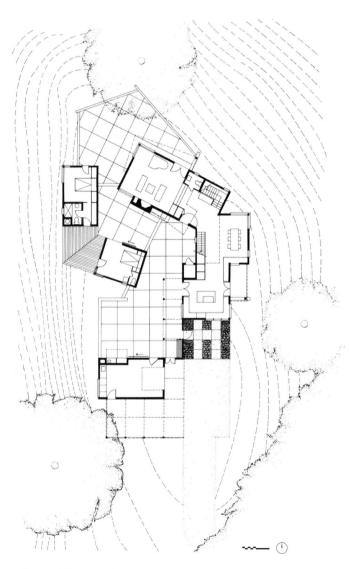

Floor plan / site plan showing
indoor and outdoor rooms

The Douro Valley, Portugal

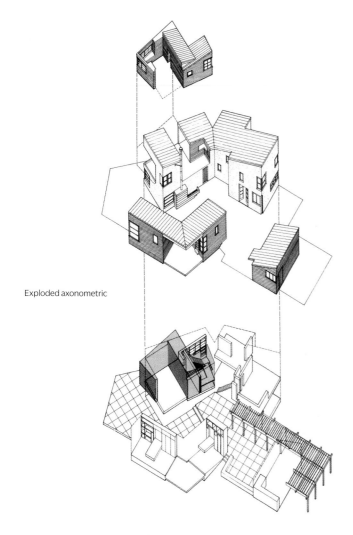

Exploded axonometric

"Bucket of Blood"
Clyde Park, Montana, 2003–2008

This is another project that was dogged by a single, overriding question: would it be possible to design and build a getaway in rural Montana that was affordable, sustainable, and respected the land and the Montana way of life?

Although the construction industry in Montana is booming, buoyed by the demand for second homes, the state's small towns are suffering. While ranchettes known pejoratively as "twenties" (tiny twenty-acre suburban parcels) increasingly impinge on agricultural land, towns that struggle to service the agrarian sprawl often see little economic reward. Cognizant of this, we opted to rehabilitate rather than build anew on open land. My family and I settled on Clyde Park, a small "cattle town" just north of Livingston, and bought a rundown commercial building sandwiched between the butcher shop and the grocery store on Miles Street, the main thoroughfare. When we first purchased the property, the facade was a chocolate brown and the interior was divided into a series of low dark spaces ending in a room-sized concrete vault. Originally constructed around 1910 as a branch bank, the 20-by-50-foot building boasted a colorful history, having also served as a health club, a gambling den, a barbershop, and a bordello. By some accounts, the latter three programs were concurrent. At that time, the title search of the property, among several names, listed the building as the "Bucket of Blood." Most recently it had been a pinball machine repair shop.

We adopted an urban live/work paradigm, which in this case would combine the needs of an architect and fly fisherman for a field office and a family getaway. The side and rear walls could not be penetrated; light had to come from the street side or by manipulating the roof. The design challenge was to figure out how to accommodate separate activities while sharing light, space, and views. Once we removed the two false ceilings and the interior partitions, we discovered a structurally sketchy truss. We replaced the truss with a simple clear span to open up the space. Enough lumber was salvaged from the demolition to nearly complete the project.

Two lofts, one at either end of the space, accommodated the live/work program. The loft on the street side is zoned for work and the one at the rear for living. Both lofts are framed with pair 2x8 Douglas fir joists salvaged from the existing structure. To make the division between church and state clear, each is accessed via a separate run of an asymmetric, bifurcated stair. Made with steel stringers and wood treads, the stairs meet in the middle across from the wood stove. The roof at the rear is lifted up over the living area to bring in light and afford a view of the Crazy Mountains. On top of the vault is a cribbing-clad bedroom, the "bird blind." The plan, completely open on the ground floor, allows for a somewhat unorthodox mix of work and play. The vault at the rear serves as an all-purpose storage container for everything from soup to chainsaws. A vintage Airstream trailer in the rear yard serves as the bunkroom/guestroom.

All the homestead's exposed framing, including the stair treads, was recycled from prior renovations of the building. The original maple flooring was also retained, including traces of former use. Inspiration for the red and green color accents was drawn from the cheering spots of color found in the stark, expansive winter landscape and in the vibrant lichen of small stones. Much of the furniture was locally made from reclaimed wood. The exterior materials are modest and durable, to address severe weather in this no-nonsense character of this rural town: asphalt shingles, commercial metal siding, Cor-ten roof, and painted-wood windows.

The final project cost was a bit more than a pickup with all the extras and significantly less than a Winnebago. What we lost in terms of rural solitude was gained in terms of sustainability, affordability, and community.

Before the renovation

Clyde Park, Montana

Reverse dormer captures light and
views of the Crazy Mountains

139

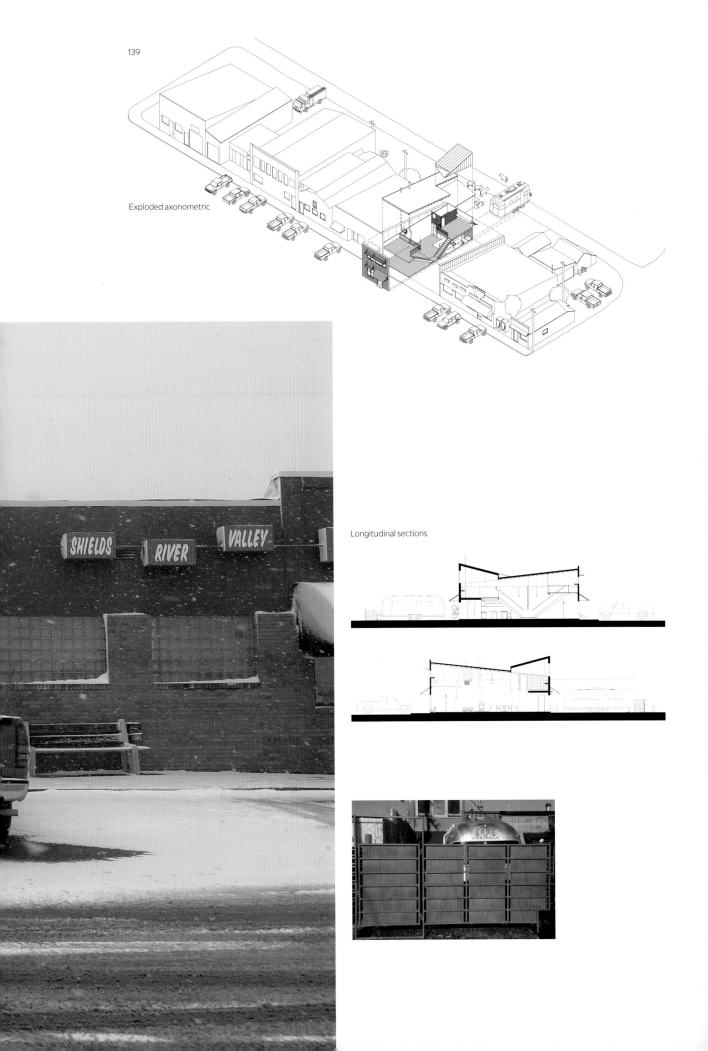

Exploded axonometric

Longitudinal sections

Shields River Valley

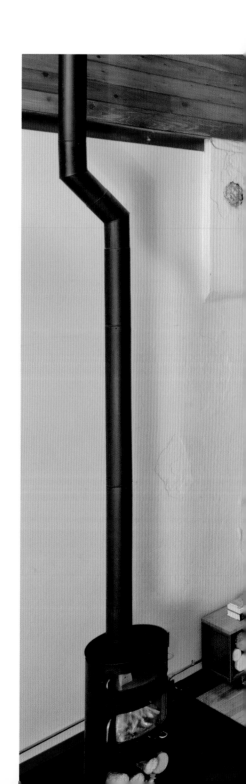

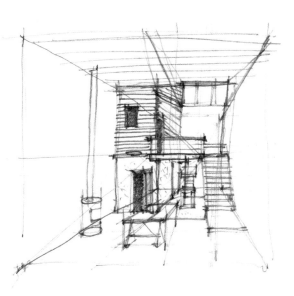

Big House / Garage House
Nonquitt, Massachusetts, 2003–2006

The Nonquitt Compound presented successive challenges. The first and most intimidating was the renovation of the "Big House," a leviathan of a residence. The house was originally built for Robert Swain Gifford, a nineteenth-century landscape painter who was a contemporary of Winslow Homer and an ancestor of one of our clients.

Loved but in poor repair when we found it, the house is sited right on Buzzards Bay in Massachusetts. Little had been done since a service wing was added in the early 1900s. The clients, environmentalists and modern art enthusiasts, were torn between conflicting desires to respect tradition and to create a contemporary residence suited to their family. Beyond the domestic needs of a large family and the specific requirements of exhibiting their art collection, our clients were keen on having the building conserve energy. Specifically, they were interested in seeing if the house could be naturally ventilated—something seldom heard of on the coast.

Fortunately, there were reliable cooling breezes from the west. That end of the house, however, was completely blocked up by the service addition. Our solution was to scoop out the service wing (a warren of cellular spaces) and thread a circulation route from the house's windward side up through the building, ultimately penetrating the roof as a belvedere that functions as a thermal chimney. Metaphorically, we thought of this as a harpoon penetrating the whale. Initiating the flow of air through this space, a "gill" was also added at the bottom of the stairs as a series of exterior louvers cocked to the prevailing breeze. However flawed our cetological metaphor, our ventilation strategy not only succeeded in cooling the house, but also helped resolve the tension between tradition and innovation: the shell of the house (the whale) retained the traditional nineteenth-century detailing, while the new circulation route was expressed utilizing a modernist vocabulary.

The "Garage House" is a modestly scaled newcomer adjacent to the Big House. Technically a remodel, the house occupies the footprint of a garage/apartment it replaced. Although in the short run, the Garage House is intended to serve as a guesthouse, in the long term, it will be an independent residence for their family. The challenge here was to maintain a connection both visually and spatially to the Big House, while simultaneously developing an identity of its own. Privacy between the houses was important, but so was the ability of the houses to function as one on occasion. Our task of finding a common language was facilitated by the approach we took in remodeling the Big House, in which we collaged new and traditional elements together. Thus, we had already established a contemporary language to complement the traditional context of the compound.

There was never any question that the Garage House would be made from materials common to the coast: wood, copper, and stone. Wood with a variety of finishes, profiles, and textures was used to relate the Garage House to the Big House, but also to distinguish the two from each other. Painted, stained, and natural surfaces play off each other to create warmth and establish a distinctive architectural character, while at the same time allowing the Garage House to recede into the landscape.

The Garage House is split into two pieces that are linked by a colonnade, creating a kind of back of house that includes a rear entry, outdoor shower, screened porch, and fireplace. The colonnade gestures toward the Big House and encloses a large outdoor room that ties the two houses together. From this outdoor room, glimpses of the water can be seen on either side of the Big House, while the colonnade screens both the Big and Garage Houses from a neighboring drive to the south. Sliding louvered doors can be opened to let in cooling breezes.

The nineteenth-century sunken garden between the houses offered a clue in understanding the microclimate

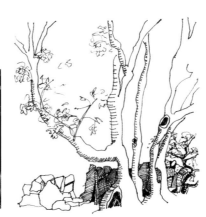

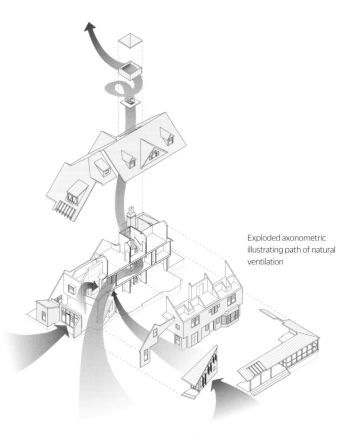

Exploded axonometric illustrating path of natural ventilation

Stone wall research field
trip, Martha's Vineyard

Cooling breezes enter
through a gill and are
drawn up the stair and
through the house by
the thermal chimney

Site plan showing the ground
floor of both the Big House and
Garage House

Our clients, former gallery owners and serious art collectors, wanted to build a small studio and an energy-efficient house in the country that would also function as their private gallery. To our surprise, we learned that we were selected in part because one of our projects, the Anderson/Ayers House (see page 118), reminded them of the playful collage of buildings and materials on the 400-year-old farm that one of them had grown up on. The house is in the Santa Ynez Valley in Southern California near Santa Barbara, where the climate is Mediterranean. The area in which we could build was quite restricted. Strong breezes from the west make for surprisingly cool afternoons and evenings. The site is exposed and can be viewed from various neighboring properties in the hilly terrain, which raised serious concerns about visibility within the local planning authority.

     Notched into a narrow bench carved into a steep hillside, the house was conceived as a device to connect to the landscape: openings frame views of the sculptural native oaks through to distant Mount Figueroa and blur the distinction between indoor and outdoor rooms. The main volume is an east-west oriented wedge that functions as a continuous dining/living/gallery space. The kitchen wing and master bedroom wing pierce this wedge and extend out to form protected courtyards to the north and south. The studio stands free of the main structure and defines and shelters the entry. Steel grating shades outdoor rooms, and operable wood screens provide shelter from western winds. Exterior shading, combined with thin building sections and generous openings, keeps the house cool in the summer. Combined with site walls and trellis structures, the landscaping — composed of drought-tolerant natives — further defines the outdoor rooms and makes a gradual transition into the natural landscape. Collaboratively chosen by the architects and clients, the colors of the stucco wedge and wood outshoots, which are not shy, were all derived from the site geology and natural vegetation. The fragmented massing, the weaving together of new and existing vegetation, and the colors inspired by the larger landscape camouflage the house at a distance and satisfied the planning issues.

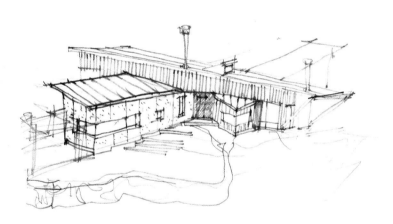

Snell/Sanders House
Santa Ynez, California, 2003–2010

Collaborating on site with the clients

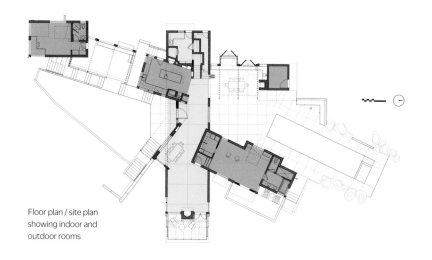

Floor plan / site plan
showing indoor and
outdoor rooms

Savannah House
Contra Costa County, California, 2004–2008

Sited in an oak savannah, just beyond the manicured sprawl of suburbia, this house stretches out like a snake along the contours of the East Bay hills of Northern California. As the house wends and winds between the dwarf oaks that cover a north-facing slope, it finds patches of sun and catches stunning distant views. Visible between the trees of the hillside forest, Mount Diablo rises to the east, a visual magnet. Summers here are hot and winters are mild. There are reliable, cooling up-valley breezes much of the year. You want to be outside.

A robust family of five with roots in South Africa, the clients were accustomed to outdoor living and wanted a house that would facilitate their lifestyle. The family moves freely between the indoors and outdoors; we came to see their home as a "base camp." They cook nearly as often on the outside grill as they do on the kitchen range. Being exposed to the Mount Diablo views and feeling connected to the land were also high priorities. Though the house needed to be large enough to accommodate a big family, we felt that on this relatively exposed site, next to protected open space, the house should be recessive and serve as a backdrop to the memorable landscape.

The combination of these desires quickly led to a linear plan that clings to the contours of the site and coils around the stand of oaks. A continuous outdoor room is carved out on the uphill side of the house. The house wraps around the slope under a single roof with deep eaves that create shelter, dip for sun protection, and rise for views. The thin section facilitates daylighting, solar gain, natural ventilation, and views in multiple directions. This undulating shed partially encloses a southern, uphill courtyard that is the primary living space, onto which all major interior spaces open. The family, like sandpipers at the edge of the surf, constantly move in and out, sitting, eating, cooking, showering, and sleeping, depending on the time of day and the time of year.

Section at south elevation

Hedgerow house at Sea Ranch, California

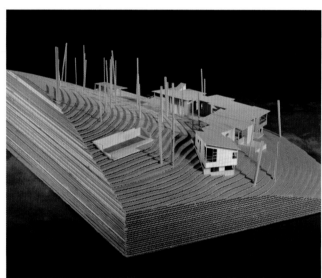

Floor plan / site plan showing
indoor and outdoor rooms

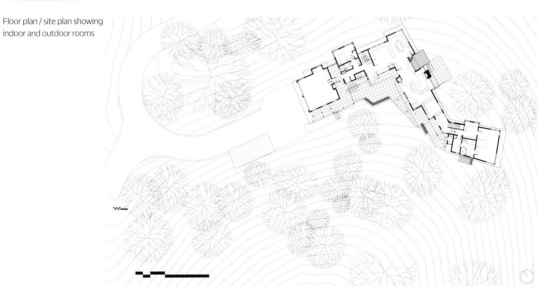

Carved into a limestone bench, this house sits on the eastern shore of the Hudson River, just above the train station in the hamlet of Rhinecliff, New York. The house is a reconversion; the design returns the 1860s Victorian farmhouse, previously broken up into a warren of small apartments, back to a single-family residence. While the traditional street facade had been maintained, the original house had been encrusted with a number of barnacle-like additions over the years. The architectural vernacular of the house became increasingly ad hoc and improvisational as the house stepped down the slope and contrived to steal views of the Hudson. With its traditional facade and disreputable back, the house was sporting a kind of architectural mullet.

Similarly motivated to take advantage of the endlessly captivating views of life on the river and mountains beyond, we also adopted an ad hoc architectural strategy. Our solution was part preservation, part renovation, part addition, and part demolition. We treated the original house as a "found object" and reinvented it, expressing what was old as old, and what was new as new. Some barnacles were scraped off, others were rebuilt, and a contemporary one was added. Design of the landscape was similarly informed by prior acts: existing stone retaining walls were reinvented and new ones added.

Along with spectacular views over the river and proximity to the rail line came serious environmental issues in terms of sound, solar gain, and glare. The zinc-clad western barnacle mitigates these issues while maximizing views of the water. These west-facing windows combat noise, glare, and solar gain by incorporating dual window systems and operable exterior shading devices. The renovation also introduces abundant light and natural ventilation throughout the house.

Barnacle House
Rhinecliff, New York, 2007–2009

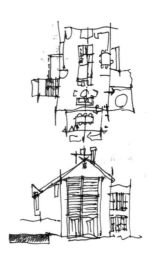

Site plan

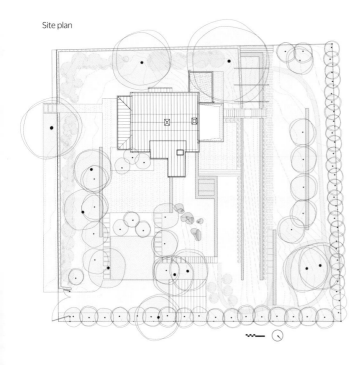

Street elevation with restored facade and modified entry

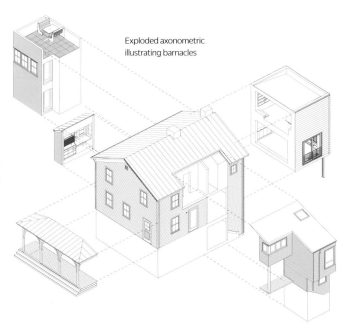

Exploded axonometric
illustrating barnacles

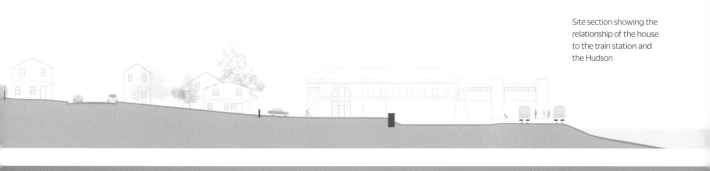

Site section showing the
relationship of the house
to the train station and
the Hudson

Wedge House
Palo Alto, California, 2009–2014

This slender residence is slid between large houses on big lots. It fills one leg of an L-shaped site, with frontage on two streets, in an established neighborhood in Palo Alto. Our clients, who live in a three-story Victorian on the other leg of the L, where they had raised their family, hired us to design them a new house. This was initially intended to accommodate their extended family; however, over the course of the process, it gradually became clear that the new building would ultimately replace the Victorian as the couple's residence. For now both houses remain in the family, connected by a casual landscape of decomposed granite, olive trees, and concrete.

The house is triangular in section and takes the shape of a wedge, but metaphorically it acts as much to connect as to cleave. It bridges a series of oppositions: architecture versus landscape, light versus shade, comfort versus climate awareness, the warmth of wood against the coolness of steel and concrete.

Single story at the street, you can reach up and touch the rain gutter at the entry. As you move through the house, spaces are organized from public to private. The kitchen looks onto the front yard, a kitchen-garden with built-in bench seating, fruit trees, and raised beds. In suburbia, this area would traditionally be given over to landscape buffer, but here, the walled kitchen-garden is turned into a room; a place to have a quiet breakfast or entertain a few friends.

Beyond the kitchen, the living room, library, and games room enclose a shaded courtyard carved out of the center of the wedge. Folding walls, when opened, seamlessly integrate the interior court with these adjacent rooms. Upstairs, a tree-fort-like master bedroom overlooks the central courtyard. Below grade, a sound studio and bedroom are day-lit by light wells. The passage to this subterranean space is illuminated by windows, skylights, and glass cylinders set into the polished concrete floor. At the rear of the site is the sculpture garden and boules courtyard.

The Wedge House is a study in the natural properties of wood; a study that unfolds over time. We have often used solid or semi-transparent stain in our work to contrast with or tease out the natural properties of wood (hue, texture, grain). The Wedge House strategy is more patient and subtle by relying on weathering and the natural characteristics of wood to develop contrasts and affinities. The Douglas fir ceiling plane extends out to the eave. Gradually, the fir will darken to a reddish color, warming the interior and harmonizing with the Alaskan yellow cedar "knuckle" that defines the entry, wraps both the pantry and the inglenook bench, and that will also deepen in hue. The outside of the house is clad with zinc siding and Kebony, an infused wood that weathers to a cool grey. Silver-blue Lodgepole "Beetle Kill" pine walls extend the line of the Kebony siding into the interior. The "Beetle Kill" is salvaged from the forests of Montana, which have been devastated by an insect blight, leaving the wood with blue-tinted streaks. Over time, the warm brown tones of the Kebony will fade to a silver patina, slowly aligning in tone to the zinc and to the Beetle Kill and visually uniting indoor and outdoor rooms.

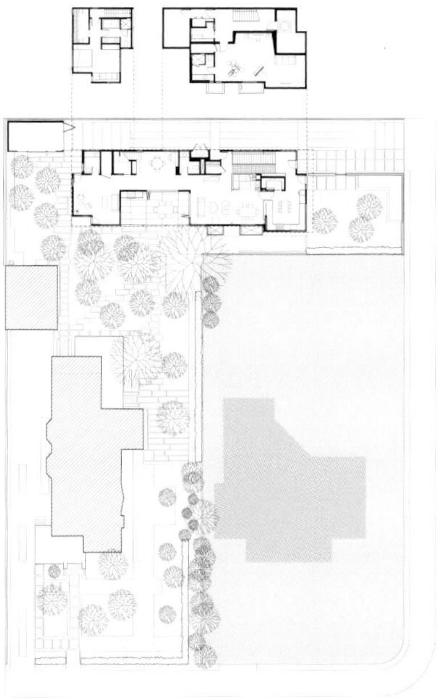

Floor plan / site plan showing indoor and outdoor rooms, with second floor and basement plans above

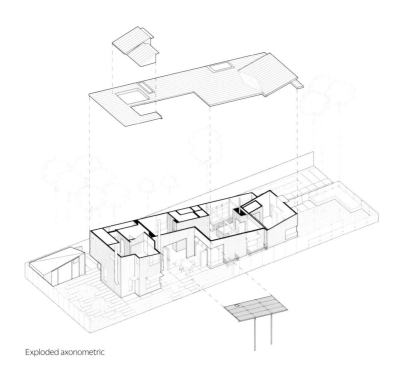

Exploded axonometric

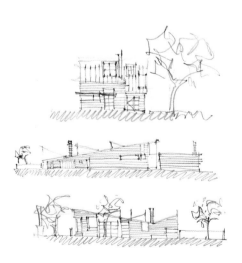

Afterword
Daniel P. Gregory

To hijack a famous statement by Lewis Mumford, the architecture of Fernau + Hartman "both belongs to the region and transcends the region." Mumford was speaking of architects of the Bay Region style like Bernard Maybeck and William Wurster. Like them, Richard Fernau and Laura Hartman, whom I have known since our days in graduate school, find inspiration in regional traditions—though "regional" means wherever they work, whether in California, Colorado, Montana, or Massachusetts. As Beth Dunlop writes, when Richard and Laura start a job, they frequently say, "Let's take a walk around." But they are not constrained by the past. They research and then they reinvent. "Walking around" is a form of exploration and discovery.

It would be odd if the Bay Region style didn't have some effect on their work, because iconic regional architecture has been their spinach—or is it kale?—from the start. Both attended architecture school at UC Berkeley under department chairman Joe Esherick, who designed the Hedgerow Houses at the Sea Ranch and who was himself an admirer of both Maybeck and Louis Kahn, i.e., the regional and the modern. Laura worked briefly for Esherick's firm before partnering with Richard to set up shop in a freestanding, foliage-swathed, one-stall garage at a residential acropolis in North Berkeley that included Maybeck's landmark Pompeian Lawson House. Richard was recruited to the Berkeley faculty by Joe and they became friends as well as colleagues. In addition, an early mentor for both was Sara Holmes Boutelle, the architectural historian who wrote an early and seminal book on the architecture of Julia Morgan.

Part of Richard and Laura's aesthetic certainly derives from the flexible, environmentally aware architecture of the Bay Area, where practitioners like Maybeck and Morgan combined natural and recycled materials such as redwood with concrete and industrial sash. For example, Richard's own house incorporates a redwood trunk and updates the Arts and Crafts Berkeley tradition of the sleeping porch with a wall that slides away to let the bed move outside. This isn't so different from Jefferson's niche bed or his dumbwaiter for wine.

There is history here but invention too: architecture as contraption, or rather, as "improvisation" in Richard's words, and "serious play" in Tom Fisher's apt description. This approach makes me think yet again of Maybeck, who once advocated putting the dining table on rollers so it could be wheeled outside for alfresco meals in good weather—a harbinger of Richard's rolling indoor-outdoor beds.

But I think Richard and Laura's architectural roots also lie in Esherick's teachings, which were more about questions than answers. Joe Esherick often recalled how his uncle, the Pennsylvania sculptor Wharton Esherick, would urge him to ask about each problem: "How would a farmer do it?" There are echoes of this in Richard's long interest in what he calls "a farmer's pragmatism." Joe called his early exploration of simple barnlike shapes and modular construction a way of "packing the box." I think Richard and Laura's career has often been about "unpacking the box": finding a way of deconstructing a program into its constituent parts, as many of their compelling axonometric drawings show. In their work, each indoor and outdoor room becomes a miniature house in its own right: as window seat, stairway landing, dining bay, office alcove, or pergola.

For Richard and Laura, designing a house involves studying the site and then lifting each major room out of its "packing crate" and setting it apart—sometimes with the structure of the crate still visible. In this way, a house finds its character as both abstract and specific, universal and idiosyncratic. They design houses as a way of telling stories about settings and the people in them: a kind of immediate, three-dimensional architectural history, or in Richard's words, a "call-and-response approach." The situation calls and they respond.

In 1987 I included Laura and Richard in an exhibition at the San Francisco Arts Commission Gallery titled "Radical Regionalism: Current Bay Area Work by Five Architectural Firms." Their key feature in the show, alongside some of Laura's evocative watercolor drawings and a redwood tree stump used as a pedestal for one of their house models, was a vividly painted cart made of wood and canvas that resembled an abstracted gypsy wagon. It was a vehicle for setting the architectural imagination in motion. Exactly the point of the show: memorable architecture is a fast moving plot about place, a way of unwrapping a room and setting it down in a new context. Radically regional is both a way to belong and go beyond. Because their approach is partly improvisational you never really know what will happen next. But with Fernau + Hartman, it's always worth the wait.

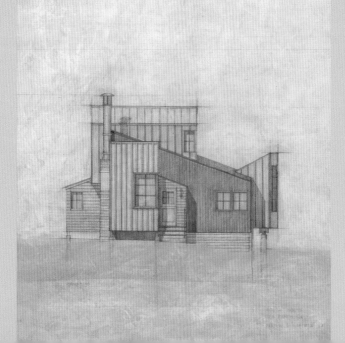

Tim Gray,
Study for cottage at Sea Ranch, California

Project credits

Anderson/Ayers House
Marin County, California
1994–1999
Project Team: Richard Fernau, Laura Hartman, Scott Donahue
(Project Architect), Susan Stoltz (Project Architect),
Anni Tilt, Keith Dubinsky, Susi Staedler, Alice Lin, Jeff Day,
Cat Chuenrudeemol, Ramon Ramierz, Alexis Masnik
Structural: MKM Associates, The Hartwell Company
Landscape: Lutsko Associates and Lazuli Art + Garden
Contractor: Kerr Construction, Peacock Designs

Avis Ranch
Park County, Montana
1996–2003
Project Team: Richard Fernau, Laura Hartman, with Project
Architects: Tom Powers (Granary House), Randy Helstern
(Granary), Aaron Thornton (Headquarters), and Sean
Gilmore, Peter Liang, Jenee Anzelone
Structural: Bridger Engineering
Landscape: Blake Nursery
Lighting: Illuminosa
Contractor: Anzick Construction

Barnacle House
Rhinecliff, New York
2007–2009
Project Team: Richard Fernau, Laura Hartman, Julia Storek
(Project Architect), Andrew Ballard (Project Architect),
John McGill, Luc Johnston, Kate Lydon, Cali Pfaff, Leyla Hilmi,
Yuki Bowman
Lighting: Eric Johnson Associates
Landscape: SCAPE Landscape Architecture
Contractor: Wolcott Builders

Berggruen House
Napa Valley, California
1986–1988
Project Team: Richard Fernau, Laura Hartman, Jim Goring
(Project Architect), Lisa Harris, Heather Schatz,
Frank Wang
Structural: Ingraham DeJesse Associates
Contractor: Beaman Construction
Special Paint Finishes: Mandy Wallace

Big House/Garage House
Nonquitt, Massachusetts
2003–2006
Main House Project Team: Richard Fernau, Laura Hartman,
Kate Biro (Project Architect), Jenee Anzelone, Peter Liang,
Andrew Benner, Rebecca Whidden, Matthew Stromberg,
Leyla Hilmi, Joe Holsen, Amber Evans, Josh Bergman
Garage House Project Team: Richard Fernau, Laura Boutelle
(Project Architect), Laura Hartman, Kate Biro, Robert
Aydlett, Anders Carpenter, Jenee Anzelone
Local Consulting Architect: David Smith–Jill Neubauer
Architects
Landscape: Stephen Stimson Associates
Lighting: Illuminosa
Contractor: Howland Company, Inc.

"Bucket of Blood"
Clyde Park, Montana
2003–2008
Project Team: Richard Fernau, Josh Bergman (Project
Architect), Peter Liang, John Victor-Faichney
Structural: Bridger Engineers
Contractor: Dave Cullen

Cheesecake Cohousing Consortium
Northern California
1990–1993
Project Team: Richard Fernau, Laura Hartman, David Kau
(Project Architect), Tim Gray, Kimberly Moses, Emily Stussi
Structural: Dennis McCroskey & Associates
Landscape: John Furtado
Contractor: Philo Saw Works

Cookhouse
Park County, Montana
2008–2012
Project Team: Richard Fernau, Laura Boutelle (Project
Architect), Laura Hartman, Andrew Ballard, Cindy Liu,
John Victor-Faichney, Ryan Metcalf
Structural: Bridger Engineering
Landscape: Blake Nursery
Contractor: Jon Evans, North Fork Builders

Fernau/Cunniff House
Berkeley, California
1990–1992
Project Team: Richard Fernau, Turk Kauffman (Project
Architect), Jenee Anzelone (Project Architect), Tim Gray,
Susan Stoltz, Scott Donahue
Structural: Bruce King
Contractor: Creative Spaces
Log erection: Paul Discoe of Joinery Structures

Laybourne House and Art Barn
Telluride, Colorado
1991–1993
Project Team: Richard Fernau, Laura Hartman, Tim Gray
(Project Architect), Anni Tilt
Structural: Peightal Guy Engineers
Contractor: Lyntrak Construction (House), Sundance
Construction (Art Barn)

Mann House
Sonoma County, California
1998–2002
Project Team: Richard Fernau, Laura Hartman, Jeff Day
(Project Architect), Alexis Masnick, Aaron Thornton,
Randy Helstern
Structural: Richard Hartwell, Jon Brody
Contractor: Jeff Nimmo, General Contractor

MV House
Martha's Vineyard, Massachusetts
1995–1998
Project Team: Richard Fernau, Laura Hartman, Susan Stoltz
(Project Architect), Keith Dubinsky, Alice Lin, Tom Powers,
Michael Roche, Alexis Masnik
Local Consulting Architect: Kate Warner
Structural: Chaloff Consulting Engineers
Contractor: Island Construction Management Co.

Newport Beach House
Newport Beach, California
1994–1997
Project Team: Richard Fernau, Laura Hartman, Tom Powers
(Project Architect), Joe Lambert (Project Architect)
Structural: Michael R. Gabriel
Interiors: Marcy Ellison
Contractor: Bibb Construction

Potomac Retreat
Eastern Panhandle, West Virginia
1996–1998
Project Team: Richard Fernau, Laura Hartman, Jeff Day (Project Architect), Alexis Masnik, Michael Roche, Don Najita, Sean Gilmore, Mary-Lynn Radych
Local Consulting Architect: Grove & Dall'Olio Architects
Structural: Structural Concepts, Inc.
Lighting: Richard Peters
Landscape: Oehme, Van Sweden & Associates, Katja Sherwood
Interiors: Andrea Marquit Clagett
Contractor: Pray Construction Company

Savannah House
Contra Costa County, California
2004–2008
Project Team: Richard Fernau, Laura Hartman, Jenee Anzelone (Project Architect), Matthew Stromberg, Josh Bergman, Anders Carpenter, Chris Peli, Chris May
Structural: Structural Solutions
Lighting: Illuminosa
Landscape: Lutsko Associates
Contractor: Diamond Construction, Don Grimoldi

Snell/Sanders House
Santa Ynez, California
2003–2010
Project Team: Richard Fernau, Laura Hartman, with Project Architects Jenee Anzelone and Laura Boutelle, Kate Lydon, Luc Johnston, Anders Carpenter, Jason Wilkinson, Julia Storek, Natalia Echeverri
Structural: Craig Dobbs
Electrical/Lighting: JMPE Electrical Engineering + Lighting Design
Landscape: Pamela Burton & Company
Contractor: Coastal Builders, Inc.

Von Stein House
Sonoma County, California
1990–1993
Project Team: Richard Fernau, Laura Hartman, Tim Gray (Project Architect), Anni Tilt, Beth Piatnitza, Emily Stussi, Geof Gainer, Scott Donahue
Structural: Lawrence Fowler & Associates
Lighting: O'Mahoney & Myer
Contractor: Fine Carpentry, Inc.

Wedge House
Palo Alto, California
2009–2014
Project Team: Richard Fernau, Laura Boutelle (Project Architect), Cindy Liu, Andrew Ballard, John Victor-Faichney, Maria Carrizosa, Brennan Stevenson, Ben Walker, Colleen Paz, Ryan Metcalf, Anastasia Yee, Laura Hartman
Structural: Fratessa Forbes Wong Structural Engineers
Lighting: Eric Johnson Associates, Inc.
Acoustics: Charles Salter Associates
Landscape: Daphne Edwards Landscape Architecture
Interior: Turnbull Griffin Haesloop (Margaret Turnbull)
Contractor: Pete Moffat Construction, Inc., IronGrain (steel work)

Photography credits

© Peter Aaron: 82; © James Balog: 50 bottom; © Richard Barnes: 4, 5, 35, 38, 39 bottom, 40, 43, 44 bottom, 45 middle, 46, 90 bottom right, 96, 98, 99, 100 top left, 101 top, 102–104, 105 bottom, 105 top left, 110, 113, 114 bottom, 115–118, 121 bottom, 122, 125 top, 152, 157, 158 bottom, 159, 172–195, 202; © Marion Brenner: 154 bottom, 155 bottom, 155 middle, 156, 158 top, 160, 161 top, 204–205; © Mark Darley/Esto: 6, 24, 27, 29 top right, 30, 31, 51 top right, 56, 207; © David Fenton: 140 bottom, 140 top left; © Tim Hursley: 84, 88 bottom, 91, 92 bottom, 93 top; © JK Lawrence: 89, 93 bottom left, 94 top, 95 top, 136, 141; © John Linden: 58–60, 61 bottom, 62–65, 126, 128, 131–135; © Gary Nafis: 165 top right; © Prakash Patel: 76, 79, 80 bottom, 81, 83; © Undine Prohl: 22, 48, 54–55; © Sharon Risedorph: 19 left, 162, 165 bottom, 167 top, 168–170, 171; © Cesar Rubio: 29 bottom left, 34 middle right, 36 bottom left, 36 bottom right, 37 bottom left, 37 bottom right, 39 top left, 44 top, 47, 50 top, 57 left, 61 top, 70 middle right, 70 top, 80 top, 90 bottom left, 100 bottom, 112, 123 top, 125 bottom, 130 top left, 130 top right, 149 top, 155 top, 166 bottom, 166 top; © Timothy Sakamoto: 16 bottom; © Peter Vanderwarker: 2, 32, 37 top, 39 top right, 66–68, 71–75, 142, 144, 145 bottom, 147–148, 149 bottom, 150–151; © Lewis Watts: 39 middle left; © Alan Weintraub: 17 bottom; © Jim Wilson/ *The New York Times*/Redux: 86–87.

Artwork credits

Running Fence © Christo and Jeanne-Claude: 10; © Tim Gray: 197; © Laura Hartman: 14, 57 right, 120 top left; © Richard Fernau: 107; Victor Hugo, *Tache* © BnF: 12; Pablo Picasso, *Mandolin and Clarinet* © 2015 Estate of Pablo Picasso/ Artist Rights Society (ARS), New York: 119 left; Robert Rauschenberg, *First Landing Jump* © Robert Rauschenberg Foundation/Licensed by VAGA, New York, NY: 16 top right; Kurt Schwitters, *Cherry Picture* © 2015 Artist Rights Society (ARS), New York/VG Bild-Kunst, Bonn: 16 top left.

All sketches © Richard Fernau

All other photographs and drawings © Fernau + Hartman Architects

This book is dedicated to Sarah, Owen, and Eliot, for their support and encouragement.

I am enduringly grateful to:

Char and Shep for opening my eyes to the visual world on the streets of Chicago. The State of California for making my extraordinary education at UC Santa Cruz and UC Berkeley possible and something I could afford. At Santa Cruz: Professor Mary Holmes for explaining the difference between an academic and a philosophical carpenter; Professor Jasper Rose for making the mystery of architecture tangible and letting the ashes fall where they would; and Professor Maurice Natanson for disclosing philosophy in the things themselves.

At Berkeley I would like to thank, in particular, Joe Esherick for giving me a start, a vague sense of direction, and for sharing fish stories; Jerry Weisbach and Richard Bender for their insight and encouragement; Marvin Buchanan for showing me how to push the pencil. The Architecture Department for supporting my creative work and research efforts with a series of mini-grants that allowed me to hire a string of research assistants without whose help and encouragement this project would have rolled to the bottom of the hill and stayed there. My design students for teaching me a thing or two and for being game. Special thanks goes to the students in my "Monograph and Manifestoes" seminar, whose ferocious intellects and unforgiving criticism sharpened my critique, steeled my courage, and ultimately toughened my hide sufficiently to undertake this project. And to all my colleagues at Berkeley and throughout the profession for setting the bar high.

To all our collaborators at Fernau + Hartman for sharing their talents and abilities and for helping give shape to a sensibility. Laura Hartman her for prodigious artistic gifts, her friendship, her patience, for not losing her accent (completely), and for being there throughout. And the talented Laura Boutelle for her refined sensibility, attention to detail, and elephantine memory. Chuck Davis, Fernau + Hartman's foster parent, for generously taking us on as architectural wards, sharing his "war stories," and instilling in us a sense of the Bay tradition one detail at a time. All our clients, our co-collaborators, whose desires and creative impulses are evident in every project in the book. They not only made the projects possible, they made them better. Finally, our consultants for keeping us out of trouble and our builders for reading between the lines and showing us the "other way to do that . . ."

To The Monacelli Press and Stacee Lawrence for giving us this opportunity. Our editor, Alan Rapp, for giving us just the right amount of direction and applying just the right amount pressure. Beth Dunlop, for her insight and guidance, and for saying "this is really a book." Tom Fisher and Dan Gregory for their critical minds and generous spirits, and for finding qualities in the work of which we were only dimly aware. Our photographers for making us look good (and for their patience). David Blankenship (a supreme collaborator) for his crisp yet provocative design and for being indefatigable.

Finally, the core collaborators: the monograph team. First, special mention must be made of Anastasia Yee for insisting on a hard cover for the mock-up and convincing me that we were close. I am particularly grateful to Ellie Ratcliff, with whom I have worked shoulder to shoulder for the last year, without whose writing and editing skills, critical judgment, and massive powers of organization the book wouldn't have happened. Nor would it have been anywhere near as resolved without the graphic eye and layout savvy of the every calm Timon Covelli.

Sara Boutelle for always knowing what to do and say. Martin Filler for everything he has written, his timely suggestions, and career long friendship.

Richard Fernau

Ackerman, Diane. *Deep Play*. New York: Vintage Books.

Beardsley, John, and Alvia Wardlaw. *The Quilts of Gee's Bend*. Atlanta: Tinwood Books, in association with The Museum of Fine Arts, Houston, 2002.

Brook, Peter. *The Empty Space*. New York: Atheneum, 1968.

Buchanan, Peter. *Ten Shades of Green: Architecture and the Natural World*. New York: The Architectural League of New York, 2005.

Butler, Samuel. *The Way of All Flesh*. London: Penguin Books, 1947.

Fernau, Richard. "Solar Architecture: A New Regionalism." *Werk-Architese* (vol. 65), 1978.

Gabbard, Krin. *Jazz Among the Discourses*. Raleigh: Duke University Press, 1995.

Harrison, Jim. *True North*. New York: Grove Press, 2004.

Hopps, Walter. *Robert Rauschenberg: A Retrospective*. New York: Guggenheim Museum, 1997.

Huizinga, Johan. *Homo Ludens: A Study of the Play-Element in Culture*. Boston: Beacon Press, 1955.

Johnstone, Keith. *Impro: Improvisation and the Theatre*. New York: Theatre Art Books, 1979.

Keeler, Charles. *The Simple Home*. Santa Barbara: Peregrine Smith, Inc., 1979.

Kernfeld, Barry. "Improvisation." *The New Grove Dictionary of Jazz*. New York: St. Martin's Press, 1988.

Melville, Herman. *Moby-Dick*. Berkeley and Los Angeles: University of California Press, 1979 [1851].

Mumford, Lewis. "The Sky Line." *The New Yorker*. October 11, 1947.

Mumford, Lewis. "The Architecture of the Bay Region." *Domestic Architecture of the San Francisco Bay Region* (San Francisco: San Francisco Museum of Art, 1949.

Riess, Suzanne. *Joseph Esherick, An Oral History: An Architectural Practice in the San Francisco Bay Area, 1938–1996*. Berkeley: Regional Oral History, Bancroft Library, University of California, 1996.

Rodari, Florian and Anne Philbin. *Shadows of a Hand: the Drawings of Victor Hugo*. London and New York: The Drawing Center in association with Merrell Holberton Publishers, 1998.

Rodari, Florian. *Collage: Pasted, Cut, and Torn Papers*. New York: Rizzoli International Publications, Inc., 1988.

Schultz, Isabel. *Kurt Schwitters, Color and Collage*. New Haven and London: Yale University Press, 2010.

Spolin, Viola. *Improvisation for the Theater and Directing Techniques*. Evanston: Northwestern University Press, 1963.

Tomkins, Calvin, and David Bourdon. *Christo: Running Fence. Sonoma and Marin Counties, California, 1972–76*. New York: Harry N. Abrams, Inc., 1978.

Tomkins, Calvin. *The Bride and the Bachelors*. New York: Penguin Group, 1968.

Tomkins, Calvin. *Off the Wall: A Portrait of Robert Rauschenberg*. New York: Picador, 2005.

Welty, Eudora. "Place in Fiction." *The Eye of the Story*. New York: Vintage Books, 1979.

Wilde, Oscar. "The Decay of Lying." *Intentions*. London: Methuen, 1921.

Woodbridge, Sally. *Bernard Maybeck: Visionary Architect*. New York: Abbeville Press Publishers, 1992.

Yosida, Shin-Ichiro and Dai Williams. *Riches from Rags: Saki-ori and Other Recycling Traditions in Japanese Rural Clothing*. San Francisco: San Francisco Craft and Folk Art Museum, 1994.

Contributors

Richard Fernau is a professor emeritus in the architecture department at the University of California, Berkeley. With an undergraduate degree in philosophy, he graduated with an architecture degree from Berkeley, after which he worked in Switzerland and traveled extensively on a fellowship in Europe and across the United States studying vernacular architecture. After gaining national attention for a variety of independent projects, he began teaching full-time and formed an architectural partnership with Laura Hartman in 1981. In 1995 he was made a Fellow of the AIA. In addition to the Fernau + Hartman office in California, he has a storefront studio in rural Montana where he pursues special projects, spends time with his wife and two sons, and fly fishes.

Laura Hartman is partner at Fernau + Hartman. She had previously worked at EHDD in San Francisco and at Dolf Schneibli Associatti in Switzerland. Though her professional life has primarily been committed to architectural practice, she has also taught at the University of California, Berkeley, the University of Oregon, and the University of Utah. Throughout her career she has maintained a dialogue between her architectural practice and art-making, conducting ongoing explorations common to both practices. Having professional, artistic, and academic interests in vernacular architecture, she is currently investigating the mining structures of Appalachia.

Beth Dunlop is editor of *MODERN* Magazine and an architecture critic and writer. The longtime architecture critic of *The Miami Herald,* she is also the author of numerous books on architecture and design. She has contributed to a wide range of national magazines and was editor-in-chief of *HOME Miami, HOME Fort Lauderdale,* and the online-only *HOME Los Angeles.* She is a graduate of Vassar College and lives in Miami Beach with her husband and a golden doodle, Oliver.

Thomas Fisher is a Professor in the School of Architecture and Dean of the College of Design at the University of Minnesota. A graduate of Cornell University in architecture and Case Western Reserve University in intellectual history, he is the author of nine books, including *In the Scheme of Things: Alternative Thinking on the Practice of Architecture, Ethics for Architects: 50 Dilemmas of Professional Practice,* and *Some Possible Futures, Design Thinking Our Way to a More Resilient World,* as well as monographs on the work of architect David Salmela and Lake|Flato. His current research involves looking at the implications of the "Third Industrial Revolution" on architecture and cities in the twenty-first century.

Daniel P. Gregory is the Editor-in-Chief of Houseplans.com, the largest online source of architectural home plans. Previously he was the Senior Home Editor of *Sunset* magazine. He holds a PhD in architectural history from University of California, Berkeley and is the author of *Cliff May and the Modern Ranch House,* and *From The Land: The Architecture of Backen, Gillam & Kroeger,* as well as numerous essays about California architects, including William Wurster and Joseph Esherick.